Making Meaning®

THIRD EDITION

Center for the Collaborative Classroom wishes to thank the following authors, agents, and publishers for their permission to reprint materials included in this program. Every effort has been made to trace the ownership of copyrighted material and to make full acknowledgment of its use. If errors or omissions have occurred, they will be corrected in subsequent printings, provided that notification is submitted in writing to the publisher.

Excerpts from *Rainforests* by James Harrison. Copyright © 2012 by Kingfisher Publications. Published in 2012 by Kingfisher, an imprint of Macmillan Children's Books, a division of Macmillan Publishers Limited. Copyright © 2012 by Macmillan Publishers Limited. Photo of Great Pyramid of Giza on p. 6 copyright © 2003–2015 Shutterstock, Inc./Andriano. Photo of funeral mask on p. 6 copyright © 2003–2015 Shutterstock, Inc./mountainpix. Photo of amulet on p. 7 copyright © Jon Bower—art and museums/Alamy. Photo of sarcophagus on p. 7 copyright © Universal Images Group Limited/ Alamy. Background art on pp. 6–7 copyright © 2003–2015 Shutterstock, Inc./diversepixel. Photo of girls playing soccer on p. 8 copyright © iStockphoto.com/amysuem. Photo of 2012 U.S. women's soccer team on p. 8 copyright © NIC BOTHMA/epa/Corbis. Photo of soccer ball on p. 8 copyright © iStockphoto.com/AtomA. Background art on pp. 8–9 copyright © iStockphoto.com/traffic_analyzer. Photo of girl on swing on p. 10 copyright © iStockphoto.com/tepic. Photo of children on p. 11 copyright © 1999–2015 Getty Images/American Images Inc. All rights reserved. Background art on pp. 10–11 © 2003–2015 Shutterstock, Inc./Kanna. Excerpts from *Great Women of the American Revolution* by Brianna Hall. Copyright © 2013 by Capstone Press. All rights reserved. Illustration copyright © Bettmann/CORBIS. Illustration courtesy of the New York Public Library: Picture Collection/Astor, Lenox and Tilden Foundation. Excerpts from *Big Cats* by Seymour Simon. Copyright © 1991 by Seymour Simon. Used by permission of HarperCollins Publishers. Excerpt from *Tuck Everlasting*. Copyright © 1975 by Natalie Babbitt. Reprinted by permission of Farrar, Straus and Giroux, LLC. All rights reserved. Excerpt from *The Van Gogh Cafe* by Cynthia Rylant. Copyright © 1995 by Cynthia Rylant. Reprinted by permission of Houghton Mifflin Company. All rights reserved. "Speech Class" from *The Place My Words Are Looking For* by Jim Daniels. Copyright © 1990 by Jim Daniels. Used by permission of Jim Daniels. "October Saturday" copyright © 1990 by Bobbi Katz. Used with permission of the author. "Eraser and School Clock" from *Canto Familiar* by Gary Soto. Copyright © 1995 by Gary Soto. Reprinted by permission of Houghton Mifflin Harcourt Publishing Company. All rights reserved. "back yard" from *All the Small Poems and Fourteen More*, by Valerie Worth. Copyright © 1987 Valerie Worth. Reprinted by permission of Farrar, Straus and Giroux, LLC. Excerpt from *Richard Wright and the Library Card* by William Miller. Text copyright © 1997 by William Miller. Permission arranged with Lee & Low Books Inc., New York, NY 10016. Excerpt from *Hurricanes* by Seymour Simon. Text copyright © 2002 Seymour Simon. Used by permission of HarperCollins Publishers. Excerpt from *Global Warming* by Seymour Simon. Text copyright © 2010 Seymour Simon. Used by permission of HarperCollins Publishers. Photos of animals on pp. 46–47 copyright © iStockphoto.com/GlobalP. Background art on pp. 46–47 copyright © 2003–2015 Shutterstock, Inc./Palau. Photo of burger meal on p. 48 copyright © 1999–2015 Getty Images, Inc./Ryan McVay. All rights reserved. Photo of pizza on p. 48 copyright © 1999–2015 Getty Images, Inc./Don Farrall. All rights reserved. Photo of cake on p. 48 copyright © iStockphoto.com/roundhill. Photo of sundae on p. 48 copyright © iStockphoto.com/skodonnell. Photo of hot dog on p. 48 copyright © iStockphoto.com/jcphoto. Photo of kids watching TV on p. 49 © 1999–2015 Getty Images, Inc./OJO Images. All rights reserved. Photo of honey on p. 49 copyright © iStockphoto.com/colevineyard. Photo of cheese and crackers on p. 49 copyright © iStockphoto.com/Elhenyo. Photo of girls on p. 50 copyright © iStockphoto.com/CEFutcher. Photo of boys on p. 51 copyright © iStockphoto.com/STEEX. Photo of cell phone on p. 52 copyright © iStockphoto.com/ leonardo255. Photo of girl using cell phone on p. 52 copyright © 2003–2015 Shutterstock, Inc./PathDoc. Photo of woman using cell phone on p. 53 copyright © 2003–2015 Shutterstock, Inc./Monkey Business Images. Border art on p. 56 copyright © 2003–2015 Shutterstock, Inc./VikaSuh. Image of train on p. 56 copyright © 2003–2014 Shutterstock, Inc./okili77. Excerpts from *A River Ran Wild*, by Lynne Cherry. Copyright ©1992 by Lynne Cherry. Reprinted by permission of Houghton Mifflin Harcourt Publishing Company. All rights reserved. Excerpt from "Mrs. Buell" from *Hey World, Here I Am!* by Jean Little. Text copyright ©1986 by Jean Little. Illustrations copyright © 1989 by Susan G. Truesdell. Used by permission of HarperCollins Publishers. "Zoo" by Edward D. Hoch, originally published in *Fantastic Universe*. Copyright © 1958 by Edward D. Hoch. Reprinted by permission of the Sternig & Byrne Literary Agency. "12 seconds from death" by Paul Dowswell reproduced from *True Stories of Heroes* by permission of Usborne Publishing, 83–85 Saffron Hill, London EC1N 8RT, UK. Copyright © 2006 Usborne Publishing Ltd. Photo of students boarding school bus on p. 94 copyright © iStockphoto.com kali9. Photo of backpack on p. 94 copyright © 2003–2015 Shutterstock, Inc./Africa Studio. Photo of children reading on p. 95 copyright © 2003–2015 Shutterstock, Inc./Diego Cervo. "Year-Round School: I'm for It" copyright © May 2005 by Chance T. Adapted and reprinted by Center for the Collaborative Classroom, 2015, by permission of *Teen Ink* magazine and TeenInk.com. Photo of smiling girl on p. 96 copyright © iStockphoto.com CEFutcher. Photo of books on p. 96 copyright © 2003–2015 Shutterstock, Inc./Aleksander Erin.Photo of family playing games on p. 97 copyright © iStockphoto.com/lisegagne. "Year Round School: I'm Against It" copyright © December 2009 by Anonymous. Adapted and reprinted by Center for the Collaborative Classroom, 2015, by permission of *Teen Ink* magazine and TeenInk.com. Photo of summer camp on p. 98 copyright © iStockphoto.com/kali9. Photo of empty desk on p. 98 copyright © 2003–2015 Shutterstock, Inc./ayzek. Photo of children building robot on p. 99 copyright © iStockphoto.com/ fstop123. Background art on pp. 98–99 copyright © 2003–2015 Shutterstock, Inc./Sakarin Sawasdinaka. "Review of *The Legend of Sleepy Hollow*" by Jennifer B. Reprinted with permission from Spaghetti® Book Club (www.spaghettibookclub.org). Copyright © 2000 Happy Medium Productions, Inc.

All articles and texts reproduced in this manual and not referenced with a credit line above were created by Center for the Collaborative Classroom.

Cover illustration by Michael Wertz, copyright © Center for the Collaborative Classroom

Center for the Collaborative Classroom
1001 Marina Village Parkway, Suite 110
Alameda, CA 94501
(800) 666-7270; fax: (510) 464-3670
collaborativeclassroom.org

ISBN 978-1-61003-711-2

Printed in the United States of America

11 12 13 BNG 24 23 22 21 20

Making Meaning®

THIRD EDITION

Think, Pair, Write

About Text Features

What expository text features did you notice? Share your thinking with your partner. Then list the features you noticed.

_____

_____

_____

_____

_____

_____

_____

_____

_____

_____

_____

_____

_____

_____

_____

_____

_____

_____

_____

_____

_____

Excerpt from *Rainforests*

by James Harrison

Rainforest resources

Tropical rainforests are home to a huge range of wildlife and plants—more than anywhere else on Earth. Yet rainforests cover only a tiny part of our planet. When rainforests disappear, so do the amazing animals and plants that live in them.

Tropical rainforest plants give us many medicines and drugs, including those used to fight cancer.

Tropical rainforests are sometimes called "the lungs of the planet." This is because the millions of rainforest trees and plants take in **carbon dioxide** and give out oxygen, which is the gas we need to breathe. Humans are pumping out too much carbon dioxide from power plants, factories, and cars.

A single rainforest tree is home to dozens of types of ants.

Too much carbon dioxide in Earth's **atmosphere** leads to **global warming**, which can change our climate. When people cut down rainforests, that leaves fewer trees to turn the carbon dioxide into oxygen. This makes the problem of global warming worse.

This pretty plant, the rosy periwinkle, is used to make drugs that treat some types of cancer. It grows in the rainforests of Madagascar.

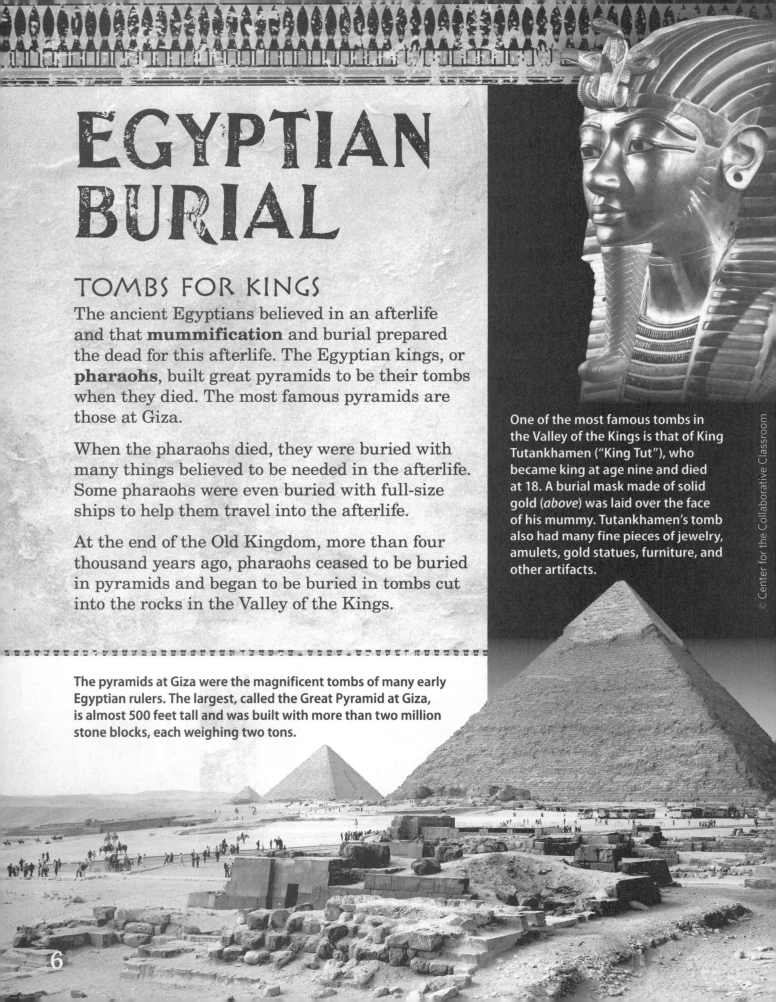

EGYPTIAN BURIAL

TOMBS FOR KINGS

The ancient Egyptians believed in an afterlife and that **mummification** and burial prepared the dead for this afterlife. The Egyptian kings, or **pharaohs**, built great pyramids to be their tombs when they died. The most famous pyramids are those at Giza.

When the pharaohs died, they were buried with many things believed to be needed in the afterlife. Some pharaohs were even buried with full-size ships to help them travel into the afterlife.

At the end of the Old Kingdom, more than four thousand years ago, pharaohs ceased to be buried in pyramids and began to be buried in tombs cut into the rocks in the Valley of the Kings.

One of the most famous tombs in the Valley of the Kings is that of King Tutankhamen ("King Tut"), who became king at age nine and died at 18. A burial mask made of solid gold (*above*) was laid over the face of his mummy. Tutankhamen's tomb also had many fine pieces of jewelry, amulets, gold statues, furniture, and other artifacts.

The pyramids at Giza were the magnificent tombs of many early Egyptian rulers. The largest, called the Great Pyramid at Giza, is almost 500 feet tall and was built with more than two million stone blocks, each weighing two tons.

MAKING A MUMMY

Mummification was the ancient Egyptian method of preserving the dead.

First, **embalmers** cleansed and purified the body and removed the vital organs. The intestines, lungs, liver, and stomach were stored in jars and buried with the deceased, while other organs (such as the brain) were simply discarded. Then the body was covered with a mineral powder that drained fluid from it, and it was left on a slanted table to drain.

Amulet

Finally, the embalmed body was wrapped in several layers of bandages. Jewels and **amulets** for protection in the afterlife were placed between the layers of bandages. The most ornate mummies were those of the kings of Egypt, the pharaohs.

The finished mummy was buried in a **sarcophagus**, a stone coffin. If the deceased was wealthy enough or was royalty, the sarcophagus was often decorated with a painted image of him.

This is the sarcophagus of Sasobek, who was the vizier (prime minister) of the northern part of Egypt during the the reign of Psammetichus I (664–610 BC).

Text by Rebecca Harlow

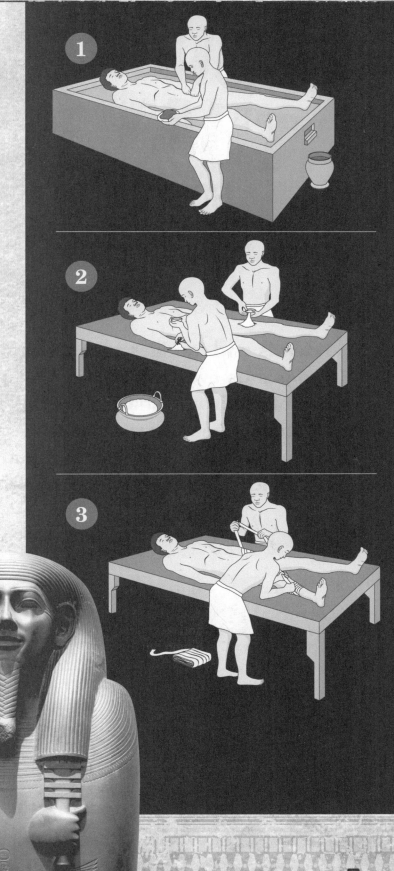

FOLLOW THAT BALL!

SOCCER CATCHING ON IN THE U.S.

Friends and families turn out in the thousands every weekend, spilling out of minivans, sharing snacks at halftime, cheering the players as they chase the black-and-white ball around the field. It's soccer mania out there!

Women are winners: American women have taken to soccer in huge numbers. Their surge in skills and confidence resulted in the U.S. women's team winning the gold medal in the 2012 Olympics.

SOCCER CONTINUES TO GROW AND GROW...

After a shaky start in its first hundred years, soccer in the United States has attracted more and more players each year. In the 12- to 17-year-old age group, one out of seven kids now plays soccer. It's an up-and-coming sport.

It's not only young people who are playing; adults are rushing to play this sport, too. Overall, around 24 million Americans of all ages play soccer. American women, especially, have made the game their own. Close to half of U.S. Youth Soccer's 3 million members are girls. In 2012, the women's U.S. Olympic team won the gold medal.

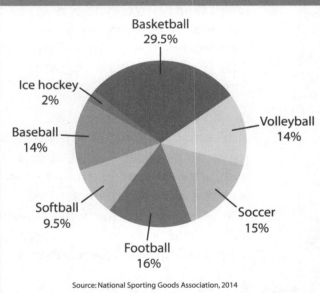

TOP SEVEN TEAM SPORTS
PLAYED BY 12- TO 17-YEAR-OLDS (2014)

Basketball 29.5%
Ice hockey 2%
Baseball 14%
Softball 9.5%
Football 16%
Soccer 15%
Volleyball 14%

Source: National Sporting Goods Association, 2014

Figures show that 12- to 17-year-old kids in the United States play a wide variety of sports.

FIVE GOOD REASONS

Why has interest and participation in soccer grown more than some other sports? There are many reasons why it has become popular.

- In football, a lineman might play several games in a row without even touching the ball. In a single soccer game, each player can touch the ball between 20 and 30 times—that's great for skill building.

- Many other sports rely on brute strength. In soccer, physical size doesn't matter as much. A player's ability has more to do with skill, stamina, and balance.

- It's a family game. Moms, dads, brothers, and sisters can all play at their own level.

- You don't need a lot of expensive equipment to play soccer.

- If soccer is played in the true spirit of the game, few players get seriously injured.

Soccer enthusiasts love the growing popularity of their favorite game. However, they have one complaint: Soccer gets nowhere near the U.S. media coverage of other sports, even the less popular ones. If major television networks decided to give soccer more airtime, who knows? In a few years, it might top the list of the most-played sports in America.

All Work and No Play

You start school at 8:00 A.M. and the day stretches out in front of you. Your class doesn't break for lunch until 11:30, and your school has removed recess from the daily schedule—so it's math and reading for the next three-and-a-half hours. What's so bad about recess? Isn't it good for students and teachers to take a break?

Trends in School Recess

More Schools Cutting Recess

More and more schools are cutting recess time or getting rid of it altogether. One out of every four elementary schools in the United States has discontinued recess for some or all grades.

Not only that: Many schools are also cutting back the time spent on subjects that are not tested, such as gym, art, and music. The main reason is so that schools can spend more time teaching academic subjects, such as math and reading. Many students are not doing well in these subjects.

And even in schools that still have recess, students get less time for breaks and PE as they move toward grade 6. There are also big differences in the amounts of recess and PE time between city and rural schools.

Why Recess Works

Students enjoy recess. They are fatigued after spending long periods of time concentrating. They see recess as important because it's a time to:

- Have a snack and a drink.
- Exercise and get rid of tension or boredom.
- Interact and catch up with their friends.

Schoolwork is hard, and sitting and concentrating puts a strain on your body and your brain. Taking even a short break from class gives your mind a chance to recharge.

Exercise at recess increases the blood supply to the brain, allowing students to concentrate on their work.

Getting some exercise at recess can also help your body make the chemicals your brain needs to help you store information. Research has shown that the brain needs to have a break every hour-and-a-half to two hours to work at its best.

Also, being able to run around and blow off steam means you're less likely to fidget during class time. When you go back to lessons after recess, you can think much more clearly and concentrate better.

Recess Restrictions

Even when a school has recess, there are often so many rules that it's hard to do more than sit and talk. Schools are worried that if a student has an accident, the school will be blamed.

- Some schools have put up "No Running" signs on playgrounds.
- Tag and ball games have been banned in many schools.
- Play equipment has been removed at some schools.

Experts agree that today, when many children spend their free time in front of the TV or computer screen, the chance to run around at recess—even for a short time—is important. It may be the only exercise a student gets all day.

Minutes of Recess Per Day

Average for city schools

Grade 3	Grade 4	Grade 5	Grade 6
23.2 mins	22.0 mins	22.0 mins	20.6 mins

Average for rural schools

Grade 3	Grade 4	Grade 5	Grade 6
29.0 mins	27.0 mins	25.5 mins	24.1 mins

Source: U.S. Department of Education, National Center for Education Statistics, Fast Response Survey System (FRSS), "Foods and Physical Activity in Public Elementary Schools: 2005," FRSS 87, 2005.

My Statements

About Recess in U.S. Schools

Looking at the bar graph on page 11, what statements can you make about recess in U.S. schools? Write your statements here.

_____

_____

_____

_____

_____

_____

_____

_____

_____

_____

_____

_____

_____

_____

_____

_____

Five Things I Learned

from the Text Features in the Excerpt

Name:

What information can you find in the text features in the excerpt on pages 14–15? Write the things you found out.

_____

_____

_____

_____

_____

_____

_____

_____

_____

_____

_____

_____

_____

_____

Excerpt from *Great Women of the American Revolution*
by Brianna Hall

Everyday Heroines

Life was difficult in Great Britain's American colonies. Women, men, and children worked hard every day just to get by. Women worked sun up to sun down caring for gardens, animals, homes, and their families

These women didn't look like rebels in their long dresses and frilly bonnets. Even on farms women wore fancy underskirts called petticoats. But when the British Parliament started passing unfair laws, colonial women had an important choice to make. Would they support King George III of Great Britain? Or would they join the fight for a new, independent nation?

Colonial women spun wool, sewed, cooked, cleaned, and looked after children. They also made household basics such as soap and candles.

parliament: a group of people who make laws and run the government in some countries

(continues)

Excerpt from *Great Women of the American Revolution*

(continued)

Who's Who in the Revolutionary War?

	Rebels	British
Major Groups	**Patriots** Colonists who disagreed with British rule and supported American independence	**Loyalists** Colonists who supported Great Britain's king
Leadership	**George Washington** Leader of the Continental army	**King George III** Ruling king of Great Britain
Armies	**Continental Army** Soldier group formed to resist British occupation, later French forces fought with the Continental army	**British Army** Considerd the most powerful army in the world at the time
Additional Forces	**Minutemen** Men who formed military forces to defend homes and towns at a minute's notice	**Mercenaries** Soldiers from other countries hired to serve with the British army

Women took risks to deliver secret messages and supplies.

heroine: a girl or woman who shows strength and courage by doing a good thing

Colonial women took action. Thousands took charge of farms and businesses when their husbands went to war. They supplied armies with bullets, food, clothing, and blankets Women crossed enemy lines with secret messages They held enemy soldiers prisoner in their homes. Thousands of women saw battle. These heroines may have appeared delicate, but they had strength inside and out. They knew that whichever side they chose, their help was needed.

Index from *Great Women of the American Revolution*
by Brianna Hall

Index

Adams, Abigail, 9
Adams, John, 9
Adulateur, The, 7
American Indians, 17

Bache, Sarah Franklin, 25
Bates, Ann, 21, 28
battles, 5, 13, 28
    Harlem Heights, 14
    Lexington and Concord, 10, 28
    Monmouth, 13
boycotts, 6, 25, 28
Brant, Molly, 17
British Parliament, 4
Burgin, Elizabeth, 18–19, 28

camp followers, 10–13, 14, 21
cannons, 11, 14, 15
Clinton, General Henry, 21
Continental Congress, 9
Corbin, Margaret, 14–15, 28

Darragh, Lydia, 22–23, 28
Daughters of Liberty, 24, 25
Declaration of Independence, 9

farms, 4, 5, 14, 24
Fort Stanwix, 17
Fort Washington, 14

Geiger, Emily, 20, 29
Greene, General Nathanael, 20

Hart, Nancy Morgan, 26–27, 29

King George III, 4, 5, 6

Ladies Association of Philadelphia, 25

mercenaries, 5
Minutemen, 5

Patterson, General John, 17
Pitcher, Molly, 13
prisoners, 5, 15, 18–19

Quakers, 22

Reed, Esther, 25
Rinker, "Mom," 21

Sampson, Deborah, 16–17, 29
slavery, 8, 9
spying, 18–19, 21, 28
Sumter, General Thomas, 20

taxes, 6

Warren, Mercy, 7
Washington, George, 5, 8, 12, 22, 23, 28
Washington, Martha, 12, 28
Wheatley, Phyllis, 8
Wilkinson, Eliza, 27
Wright, Prudence, 15

from *Big Cats* (1)
by Seymour Simon

The lion (*Panthera leo*) is sometimes called the "King of Beasts." It certainly looks the part: an adult male lion has a noble head and mane, a powerful jaw and sharp teeth, and what seems to be a dignified manner. It can weigh more than 400 pounds and be 9 to 10 feet long. But, of course, there are no "kings" among animals. The lion is no mightier or braver than any of the other big cats. It is a large and strong hunter that kills prey to get its food and survive.

Adding to the lion's "majesty," is its thunderous roar. Both males and females roar. A male lion's roar can be a way of staking out its territory and warning other lions away. Sometimes a lion will stop eating just to let loose with an earsplitting roar. A loud roar can be heard from a distance of five miles. Low roars are used by a female to call her cubs or to locate other lions. Sometimes whole groups of lions, called prides, roar together. Most of the loud group roaring takes place at night, sometimes as a response to the roars of nearby prides or solitary lions.

Most kinds of big cats are solitary—they live and hunt alone most of the time. But lions are different because they are sociable— they live in groups called "prides." A pride includes a number of lionesses and their cubs, along with several males. The members of a pride share an area together and are more or less peaceful among themselves. A pride can have as few as three or four individuals or as many as thirty-five or more. Most prides have at least twice as many females as males.

The lionesses are the core of a pride. They are usually related to each other and remain with the pride all their lives. Males stay

(continues)

with a pride from a few months to several years before they leave by themselves or are driven out by a rival male.

The lionesses share all the chores of the pride. They defend the pride area by driving away any strange females. One or more lionesses guard the cubs while the others are off hunting. The females even suckle each other's cubs, so that a cub may feed from three or four different lionesses to get a full meal. If a lioness dies, her cubs will stay with the pride and be fed by other females. Being a member of a pride is a great advantage for a lion's chance of survival.

While most of the other big cats live in dense forests, swamps, or tropical rain forests, lions usually live in wide-open plains. Only a few hundred years ago, lions roamed wild in parts of Asia and southeastern Europe. But today, their range is much smaller, limited to the central and southern parts of Africa and a small game reserve in India called Gir Forest.

Another advantage of living in a pride is that a group of lions hunting on an open plain is much more successful than a lion hunting alone. Several lions can bring down larger animals and kill more animals on a single hunt. In addition, a pride often eats all of a kill and does not need to guard the remains against hyenas or vultures.

Females usually do most of the hunting. Often, several females will stampede a herd and drive the prey into a trap where other females or males are lying in wait. Once a kill has been made, the stronger males and females eat first, while the cubs and weaker adults scramble for the remains. Sometimes males will share the kill first with cubs rather than with adult females. But when food is scarce, fighting for food can be fierce and some cubs may starve.

Excerpt from *Big Cats* by Seymour Simon. Copyright © 1991 by Seymour Simon. Used by permission of HarperCollins Publishers.

Stop and Ask Questions
About *Big Cats*

At each stop, write your questions in the box.

STOP 1

STOP 2

STOP 3

from *Big Cats* (2)
by Seymour Simon

Almost all the wild cats, big and small, have been relentlessly hunted and trapped by people. Throughout history, thousands upon thousands of tigers and lions have been hunted down in the name of sport. In the 1960s and 1970s, the demand for fur coats made from the skins of spotted cats led to widespread killing of the leopard, cheetah, and jaguar, along with smaller spotted cats such as the snow leopard and clouded leopard. The puma has also been trapped and poisoned for being a killer of livestock.

Though some of the big cats are now protected by laws in many countries, illegal killing still goes on. Of even more concern is that as more and more land is taken from the wild, there is less and less room for the big cats to live.

What can we do to save the big cats? We can support laws to stop the sale and use of wild cat skins around the world. We can help wildlife organizations and encourage governments to set up preserves where big cats will be safe. We can learn to treasure the wildlife on our planet instead of destroying it. The future of the big cats is up to us.

from *Tuck Everlasting*
by Natalie Babbitt

It was another heavy morning, already hot and breathless, but in the wood the air was cooler and smelled agreeably damp. Winnie had been no more than two slow minutes walking timidly under the interlacing branches when she wondered why she had never come here before. "Why, it's nice!" she thought with great surprise.

For the wood was full of light, entirely different from the light she was used to. It was green and amber and alive, quivering in splotches on the padded ground, fanning into sturdy stripes between the tree trunks. There were little flowers she did not recognize, white and palest blue; and endless, tangled vines; and here and there a fallen log, half rotted but soft with patches of sweet green-velvet moss.

And there were creatures everywhere. The air fairly hummed with their daybreak activity: beetles and birds and squirrels and ants, and countless other things unseen, all gentle and self-absorbed and not in the least alarming.

Stop and Ask Questions

About *Tuck Everlasting* (1)

At each stop, write your questions in the box.

STOP 1

STOP 2

STOP 3

STOP 4

STOP 5

Stop and Ask Questions

About *Tuck Everlasting* (2)

Name:

At each stop, write your questions in the box.

STOP 1

STOP 2

STOP 3

STOP 4

STOP 5

Stop and Ask Questions

About *Tuck Everlasting* (3)

At each stop, write your questions in the box.

 1

 2

STOP 3

STOP 4

 5

Stop and Ask Questions
About *Tuck Everlasting* (4)

Name:

At each stop, write your questions in the box.

 1

 2

 3

 4

Story Elements

Book title: _____

Author: _____

Main characters: _____

_____

Setting: _____

_____

_____

Plot: _____

_____

_____

Problem or conflict: _____

_____

_____

Climax: _____

_____

_____

Theme: _____

_____

_____

Stop and Ask Questions

About *The Van Gogh Cafe* (1)

At each stop, write your questions in the box.

STOP 1

STOP 2

STOP 3

© Center for the Collaborative Classroom   **Making Meaning®** | **27**

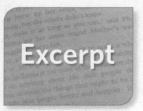

Excerpt

from *The Van Gogh Cafe*

by Cynthia Rylant

And this goes on for a while until the biggest story happens. A story that will enter quietly into the walls of the cafe and become part of its magic.

For a man whose wife has died drives through Flowers, Kansas, one morning on his way to something new. He is sad. He really isn't sure where he's going.

But passing the Van Gogh Cafe, he sees the possum. He sees the possum and he sees all the hungry animals standing beneath it, eating the scraps of muffins and potatoes.

And the man sees something else there, too, something no one has seen until now. And because of what he sees, he turns his car around and drives back where he belongs, back to his farm, which he turns into a home for stray animals, animals who come to him and take away his loneliness.

Stop and Ask Questions

About *The Van Gogh Cafe* (2)

At each stop, write your questions in the box.

STOP 1

STOP 2

STOP 3

Speech Class
(for Joe)
by Jim Daniels

We were outcasts—
you with your stutters,
me with my slurring—
and that was plenty for a friendship.

When we left class to go to the therapist
we hoped they wouldn't laugh—
took turns reminding the teacher:
"Me and Joe have to go to shpeesh clash now,"
or "M-m-me and J-Jim ha-have to go to
        s-s-speech now."

Mrs. Clark, therapist, was also god, friend, mother.
Once she took us to the zoo on a field trip:
"Aw, ya gonna go look at the monkeys?"
"Maybe they'll teach you how to talk."
We clenched teeth and went
and felt the sun and fed the animals
and we were a family of broken words.

For years we both tried so hard
and I finally learned
where to put my tongue and how to make the sounds
and graduated,
but the first time you left class without me
I felt that punch in the gut—
I felt like a deserter
and wanted you
to have my voice.

"Speech Class" from *The Place My Words Are Looking For* by Jim Daniels. Copyright © 1990 by Jim Daniels. Used by permission of Jim Daniels.

October Saturday
by Bobbi Katz

All the leaves have turned to cornflakes.
It looks as if some giant's baby brother
had tipped the box
and scattered them upon our lawn—
millions and millions of cornflakes—
crunching, crunching under our feet.
When the wind blows,
they rattle against each other,
nervously chattering.

We rake them into piles—
Dad and I.
Piles and piles of cornflakes!
A breakfast for a whole family of giants!
We do not talk much as we rake—
a word here—
a word there.
The leaves are never silent.

Inside the house my mother is packing
short sleeved shirts and faded bathing suits—
rubber clogs and flippers—
in a box marked SUMMER.

(continues)

October Saturday *(continued)*

We are raking,
Dad and I.
Raking, raking.
The sky is blue, then orange, then gray.
My arms are tired.
I am dreaming of the box marked SUMMER.

What I Read	What I Inferred
1. "millions and millions of cornflakes— crunching crunching under our feet. When the wind blows, they rattle against each other, nervously chattering."	The wind makes the leaves rub together, and it sounds like the leaves are talking.
2.	

Eraser and School Clock
by Gary Soto

My eraser
Is pink
And car-shaped.
It skids across
My math test,
Which is a mess of numbers,
All wrong, like
When I unscrewed
The back of my watch
And the workings
Fell out.
The teacher frowned
When she saw
The watch,
Its poor heart
Torn out. Now
I'm working
On my math,
And I think,
I think, I think
I know. I look
Up at the school clock
With its hammerlike tick.
I could tear
Open its back,
And perhaps
The springs and gears

(continues)

Eraser and School Clock (continued)

Would jump
And time stop.
This test could stop,
And my friends
Freeze, pencils
In their hands,
Erasers, too.
All would freeze,
Including my teacher,
And I could blow
On the skid marks
Of my eraser.
I walk out
To the playground,
My eight fingers
And two thumbs
Wrapped around
A baseball bat.
The janitor
Is frozen
To his broom,
The gardener
To his lasso of
Hose and sprinkler,
And the principal
To his walkie-talkie.
I hit homer

(continues)

Eraser and School Clock (continued)

After homer,
And they stand,
Faces frozen
And mouths open,
Their eyes maybe moving,
Maybe following
The flight
Of each sweet homer.
What a dream.
I shrug
And look around
The classroom
Of erasers and pencils,
The clock racing
My answers to the finish.

Poem

back yard
by Valerie Worth

Sun in the back yard
Grows lazy,

Dozing on the porch steps
All morning,

Getting up and nosing
About corners,

Gazing into an empty
Flowerpot,

Later easing over the grass
For a nap,

Unless
Someone hangs out the wash—

Which changes
Everything to a rush and a clap

Of wet
Cloth, and fresh wind

And sun
Wide awake in the white sheets.

from *Richard Wright and the Library Card*
by William Miller

For the most part, they were like so many white men he had known before. They would never understand a black boy who wanted a library card, a black boy who wanted to read books even they didn't read.

Only one man seemed different from the others. Jim Falk kept to himself, and the other men ignored him, as they ignored Richard. Several times, Richard had been sent to the library to check out books for him.

One day, when the other men were out to lunch, and Jim was eating alone at his desk, Richard approached him.

"I need your help," Richard said.

"Are you in some kind of trouble?" Jim asked with a suspicious look.

"I want to read books. I want to use the library, but I can't get a card," Richard said, hoping Jim would not laugh in his face.

"What do you want to read?" Jim asked cautiously. "Novels, plays, history?"

Richard felt confused. His mind was racing so fast, he couldn't think of a single book.

Jim said nothing, but reached into his desk and brought up a worn, white card. He handed it to Richard.

"How will you use it?" Jim asked.

"I'll write a note," Richard said, "like the ones you wrote when I got books for you."

"All right," Jim said nervously. "But don't tell anyone else. I don't want to get into trouble."

Excerpt from *Richard Wright and the Library Card* by William Miller. Text copyright © 1997 by William Miller. Permission arranged with Lee & Low Books Inc., New York, NY 10016

Double-entry Journal

Name:

About *Richard Wright and the Library Card*

What I Inferred

What I Read

from *Hurricanes*
by Seymour Simon

Hurricanes are the only weather disasters that have been given their own names, such as Andrew, Camille, Floyd, Fran, Hugo, Irene, Katrina, Opal, and Rita. In some ways all hurricanes are alike. But like people, each hurricane has its own story.

All hurricanes form in the same way. They begin life in the warm, moist atmosphere over tropical ocean waters. First, the atmosphere gathers heat energy through contact with ocean waters that are above 80 degrees Fahrenheit to a depth of about two hundred feet. Next, moisture evaporating from the warm waters enters the atmosphere and begins to power the infant hurricane.

The growing hurricane forms bands of clouds and winds near the ocean surface that spiral air inward. The air is heated by warm ocean water, creating strong winds and forcing them to rise higher. This increases the power of the hurricane and leads to stormy conditions over huge areas. Hurricanes can easily last more than a week and may strike Caribbean islands days before whirling north and west into the United States.

Double-entry Journal

About _____

What I Inferred

What I Read

Excerpt

from *Global Warming*
by Seymour Simon

For thousands of years, the balance of greenhouse gases in the atmosphere had not changed much. But now we burn huge amounts of coal, oil, and natural gas to generate energy. Every year, billions of tons of carbon dioxide pour out from the exhausts of cars, trains, trucks, airplanes, buses, and ships and from the chimneys of factories. There is 30 percent more carbon dioxide in the air than there was 150 years ago.

Trees, like other green plants, convert carbon dioxide into oxygen. But trees and forests are cut down in huge numbers. When wood burns or decays, even more carbon dioxide is released. Carbon dioxide enters into the atmosphere much faster than the remaining forests and oceans can absorb it.

The release of other greenhouse gases adds to the speed at which the world's climate is changing. Methane is released by millions and millions of cattle and other farm animals. Nitrous oxide comes from chemicals used in soil fertilizers, as well as from automobiles.

Excerpt from *Global Warming* by Seymour Simon. Text copyright © 2010 Seymour Simon. Used by permission of HarperCollins Publishers.

Double-entry Journal

About *Global Warming*

What I Inferred

What I Read

© Center for the Collaborative Classroom

Making Meaning® | **43**

from *Rainforests*
by James Harrison

Large areas of tropical rainforest are destroyed every day. This is partly because companies cut down trees to sell as timber. The hardwood is used to make furniture and paper. Other companies clear areas of forest so that cattle can graze there, and then they sell the meat as beef around the world. Some companies destroy areas of the rainforest so they can dig out valuable minerals lying under the ground.

Today there are roads running through many rainforests. Giant trucks carry logs, minerals, and farm animals along the roads. People build towns for the workers who come to live there. Companies build dams and pipelines that may pollute the land and the water. Many local tribes are forced to leave.

- -

Tropical rainforests are home to a huge range of wildlife and plants—more than anywhere else on Earth. Yet rainforests cover only a tiny part of our planet. When rainforests disappear, so do the amazing animals and plants that live in them.

Tropical rainforests are sometimes called "the lungs of the planet." This is because the millions of rainforest trees and plants take in carbon dioxide and give out oxygen, which is the gas we need to breathe. Humans are pumping out too much carbon dioxide from power plants, factories, and cars.

Too much carbon dioxide in Earth's atmosphere leads to global warming, which can change our climate. When people cut down

(continues)

rainforests, that leaves fewer trees to turn the carbon dioxide into oxygen. This makes the problem of global warming worse.

- -

As you read this book, tropical rainforests are shrinking. Every second, a piece of rainforest the size of a soccer field is destroyed or damaged. The future of the world's rainforests is very uncertain.

Rainforests are cut down for timber and to make large farms to grow crops and raise cattle. Companies that mine minerals and build new roads, towns, and pipelines all destroy areas of rainforest.

Today there are many campaigns to protect rainforests. One program creates reserves or parks where no one can build or clear trees to make large farms. Everyone can help rainforests by buying fair trade bananas, coffee, and cocoa, as well as wood and paper sold by companies that do not destroy the forests.

COPYCATS

Why Clone?

Cloning is a high-tech way to create a living thing that is an exact genetic copy of another. Why would we want to create identical living things? For farmers, there are many reasons. Farmers already use cloning techniques to produce desirable varieties of plants, such as apple trees that grow crisp, juicy fruit. One technique is to grow plants from cuttings taken from other plants. A plant that grows from a cutting is a clone because it has the same genetic makeup as the original plant.

In 1996, scientists succeeded in cloning the first mammal. Since then, a debate has raged about whether it is ethical or necessary to clone animals—including humans. Although the idea is controversial, some scientists believe that cloned human beings could one day become a reality. Other high-tech procedures, such as organ transplants, once faced the same kind of debate, but today they are widely performed.

In 2006, the Food and Drug Administration (FDA) reported that it was safe to eat meat from animals that had been cloned. In 2008, the FDA approved the sale of cloned-animal meat in supermarkets without requiring them to be labeled as such.

PROS

Building a Better Breed

Since the first mammal was cloned, scientists have cloned many other creatures, including cows, cats, and fruit flies. Traditionally, farmers have paired a male animal with a female and hoped that they would produce offspring with desirable traits, such as animals that have thick wool or high-quality meat. Today, farmers are starting to use cloning as a surer way to get that same result.

Protection from Extinction

Cloning might also be a way to protect endangered species from extinction. In 2005, scientists created clones of the gray wolf, a species once hunted to near extinction. Today, thanks to a U.S. protection law, gray wolves are thriving in several states, including Minnesota and Wisconsin. But if gray wolves ever become endangered again, scientists now know how to clone them so they won't become extinct.

Human Health

There are many potential advantages of cloning human beings. It might give infertile couples a chance to have children. Additionally, people who are likely to have a child with a genetic disorder might use cloning to have a better chance at producing a healthy child. Cloning could also be used to create healthy organs for people who are sick and need a transplant.

Cloning might help us understand how human genes work. This could lead to the discovery of treatments for genetic disorders such as cystic fibrosis. Discoveries like these have the potential to make many people's lives easier. These discoveries might even save lives.

CONS

Cloning for the Wrong Reasons

Where do we draw the line between the right reasons and the wrong reasons for using cloning? If human cloning is allowed in a few specific cases, people might begin to use it in other ways. For example, cloning might be used to create children who have specialized talents—such as amazing mathematical or athletic abilities—much like animals might be cloned for specific desirable traits. From there, cloning could lead to the creation of groups of people for specific purposes, such as fighting in wars. Many people argue that it is wrong to experiment with human life in this way.

Health Risks

Studying human cloning has big complications. Real human cells must be used, so if a particular experiment does not work out, the result could be a flawed copy of a human being—and that person would never have a normal life.

So far, scientists have found it difficult to produce healthy clones of mammals. For example, studies done in Japan have shown that cloned mice have poor health and die early. About a third of cloned cows have died young, and many of them were too large. Many cloned animals appear healthy at a young age but die suddenly and mysteriously. We should expect the same problems in human clones.

Even if scientists were able to produce human clones that were physically healthy, other important parts of human development might be affected. For example, a person's mood, intelligence, or sense of individuality might not develop normally.

Legal Roadblocks

In many countries it is against the law to clone a human being because of the many ethical and safety concerns. Congress is currently considering passing a law to ban human cloning in the United States.

"Junk food" is a slang term for food with little nutritional value. It includes food that is high in fat, sugar, or salt (or all three). Junk food makes up a large portion of food we see advertised on TV.

THE DEBATE ON BANNING JUNK FOOD ADS

Advertising Works

Food companies spend billions of dollars on TV advertising each year. The reason is simple: Advertising works. It's especially effective with children. A 2013 study found that the average American child sees about 13 food commercials a day, or 4,700 a year. Teens see more than 16 a day, or 5,900 a year. The study found that these kids see only about one ad per week for healthy foods such as fruits, vegetables, and bottled water. Most of the food ads they see are for junk food.

What's Junk?

Junk food may taste good, but it's low in nutritional value. For example, a sugary donut doesn't have as many nutrients as an apple. Many people argue that one way to encourage people—especially children—to choose more nutritious foods is to regulate, or control, the messages they receive about food from advertising. Others argue that regulating advertising will simply create more problems.

PROS

Good Habits Start Young

Some countries already regulate TV advertising for junk food. The people who support such regulations say that TV advertising encourages bad eating habits among young people because young people are more easily influenced than adults by advertising. In 2007, the United Kingdom started banning junk food advertising during children's TV shows. In 2011, the U.S. government proposed voluntary guidelines for food ads targeting children and teenagers. The guidelines state that foods advertised to children must include healthful ingredients and be limited in the amounts of sugar, saturated fat, trans fat, and salt they contain. The nation's largest food companies responded that the guidelines were too strict and proposed more lenient guidelines for ads.

A child who develops unhealthy habits is also likely to keep on making unhealthy choices as an adult. So it is preferable to control the messages that young people receive. This gives them a better chance at having a healthy future.

Good health is a big concern for many people today. Worldwide, hundreds of millions of people have serious problems related to an unhealthy diet, including diabetes and heart disease. A common problem in the United States is obesity: In a 2011–2012 survey, the Center for Disease Control found that about 80 million adults and about 12.5 million children were obese. Limiting junk food ads may be one way to help people make choices that will prevent obesity and other health problems.

> "In the United Kingdom, foods such as olive oil, honey, and cheese are labeled as junk food."

The United Kingdom bans junk food ads during children's TV shows and on children's channels.

CONS

Giving Food a Bad Name

There are some big problems with creating rules about junk food advertising. For example, how do we decide exactly what is junk food and what is not? In the United Kingdom, foods such as olive oil, honey, and cheese have been banned from advertising during certain hours because they are labeled "junk food." These foods have nutritional value, but they are also high in fat, salt, or sugar. Calling these foods "junk food" makes it more difficult for people to understand what makes up a healthy, balanced diet.

To make things even more complicated, some fast food companies' ads now emphasize more nutritious choices—for example, providing fruit and milk with children's meals. Some promote health and fitness, too. If all fast food ads were banned from children's TV, these healthy messages would be as well.

Some parents feel that they have the right to decide what is best for their children and that regulating TV ads takes away that right. It is up to the parent to say yes or no when a child asks for something he or she has seen advertised on TV. What the parent says helps the child learn about how advertising affects the people who see it.

Regulating TV ads takes away some of the information parents and children have access to. They need that information in order to make their own buying decisions. Making these choices is the consumer's right, not the right of the government.

All-girls and All-boys Schools: Better for Kids

Out in the world, males and females live, work, and interact with one another. But at many schools, the classrooms are filled with just boys or just girls. Life isn't separated into male and female sides, so why should schools be?

Together or Apart?

Because male and female students think, learn, and behave differently from one another, it makes sense that they would do better at schools that understand these differences. Research has shown that students at all-boys or all-girls schools are more confident and more willing to try new things, and that they might even perform better academically than students at coeducational schools.

Different Brains, Different Gains

You might not realize it, but your brain develops differently from the brain of a classmate of the opposite sex. For example, the area of a girl's brain that understands language is one of the first areas to develop. In a boy's brain, other areas develop first, such as the part that makes sense of math. Because of differences like these, males and females learn various subjects in different ways.

In 1972, a new law came into effect stating that all U.S. public schools should be coeducational. However, the law was changed in 2006 to allow all-boys and all-girls public schools.

An all-boys or all-girls school can focus its instruction to meet the needs of either male or female students, not both at the same time. This helps students make faster, stronger progress. For example, one Michigan study compared graduates of all-boys and all-girls high schools with graduates of coeducational high schools. The researchers found that male students in all-boys schools scored better in reading and writing than male graduates of coeducational schools. Likewise, female students in all-girls schools scored better in science and reading than their female peers in coed schools.

Positive Proof in Test Results

In 2008, researchers in Florida found that students in all-boys and all-girls classrooms made greater academic gains: 55 percent of boys in coed classrooms scored proficient (at or above a passing level), while 85 percent in all-boys classrooms scored proficient. Girls also saw gains: 59 percent of girls in coed classrooms scored proficient, while 75 percent in all-girls classrooms scored proficient.

In England, researchers at Cambridge University did a four-year study on the different ways that boys and girls learn. The researchers found that all-boys and all-girls classrooms were remarkably effective at boosting boys' performance, particularly in English and foreign languages, as well as improving girls' performance in math and science.

Building Confidence

Supporters of all-boys and all-girls classrooms argue that the students are less distracted in those environments. This makes it easier for all students to focus on their lessons.

Students who feel shy around people of the opposite sex could benefit the most from all-boys or all-girls schools. Without the pressure of worrying about how they might look to members of the opposite sex, they can feel free to be themselves. For example, they might explore subjects they wouldn't normally explore and join clubs or sports teams. Shy students are likely to feel more comfortable in an all-boys or all-girls class, so they're more likely to feel enthusiastic about speaking up in class, asking questions, and participating in class discussions.

Many people argue that an all-boys or all-girls education could make it more difficult for young people to learn how to relate to members of the opposite sex. It's true that we live in a world where males and females live and work with one another and are not segregated as in all-boys or all-girls schools. But many graduates of these schools say that they feel confident not only about their academic abilities, but also about their personalities. And this confidence can give graduates a head start in building friendships with the opposite sex.

Shy students may feel happier about participating in an all-boys or all-girls class. Taking part in classroom discussions helps them get more out of the lesson.

An Increasingly Popular Option

All-boys and all-girls classes and schools are gaining favor across the United States. In 2002, only a dozen or so public schools in the United States offered this option. In 2012, there were around 500 all-girls and all-boys schools. School districts, parents, and students are increasingly getting on board with all-boys and all-girls education as a great way to boost students' scores and confidence.

Do Kids **Really** Need Cell Phones?

There are nearly seven billion cell phones in use worldwide—and the trend has caught on among eight- to twelve-year-olds. With bright colors and catchy ringtones, cell phones are hard for young people to resist.

But why does a person as young as eight years old need a cell phone? He or she is likely to come up with a list of reasons, including "All my friends have them." However, for very young kids, there are many benefits to having cell phones beyond the obvious "cool" factor.

Cell Phones Are a Lifeline

In an emergency, a cell phone can be indispensable. Cell phones allow children to dial 911 or call their parents if there is an accident or emergency. Also, cell phones allow children to stay in contact with family. Children, parents, and other caregivers are often in different places throughout the day, and things often don't go as expected. For example, if soccer practice ends early or a parent is stuck in traffic, a cell phone can let everyone know how plans have changed.

As the lives of families become more and more hectic, the number of students who are alone after school is increasing. Today, the number of children in the United States with mothers in the labor force is around 70 percent. This means that many students are at home alone after school. It is more important than ever to have a way of keeping in touch with family—and a way of getting help in an emergency.

Cell phones can help the day run smoothly by keeping family members in touch with one another.

Cell Phone Use Is Easy to Limit

Many people worry that cell phones put young children in danger. Bullies or even criminals might use the phones to contact children, and the Internet access on many cell phones puts children even more at risk. There is also the chance that children would run up high cell phone charges.

However, many cell phones now have parental controls. For example, it's possible to place limits on who can call and be called with some phones, and parents can limit or block Internet access on phones. Most cell phones have a Global Positioning System (GPS) so that parents can find their child easily using another cell phone or a website.

Parents can also opt for a prepaid plan so that their children can't go over spending limits but can still call their parents if they need to. Features like these make it possible for children to get the benefits of cell phone use without the risks.

Cell Phones Promote Familiarity with Technology

Today, many jobs are dependent on cell phones and similar devices. Mobile devices such as cell phones have become just as important as the computer has been in the last 20 years. One way to ensure that young people are familiar with this technology is to allow them to use cell phones now.

Students can use a cell phone for more than just text messaging and talking. For example, cell phones can be helpful when doing schoolwork. On most cell phones, students can check the Internet for definitions and spellings of tricky words, take photos and make short videos for school projects, and listen to audiobooks. Carrying out a variety of tasks using cell phones can help

Workplaces around the world are becoming more and more reliant on technology.

boost young people's confidence around technology—and, in turn, help them feel confident when they grow up and begin working.

Cell Phones Teach Responsibility

Owning a tool such as a cell phone can be a great way for children to learn responsibility. Because cell phones are valuable and can be used in different ways, children must learn to use them wisely—for example, making sure they don't lose them, keeping them charged, and using them only when they are not in school. These things help young people learn to treat personal possessions with care. Learning responsibility in this way helps children to respect other people's belongings, too.

An Unstoppable Trend

Researchers say that about 56 percent of American preteens have cell phones. If young children don't already own cell phones, it's likely that they will in the future. The best way for young people to benefit from this technology when they grow older is to learn to use it responsibly today.

How to Make an Origami Cup

Now you can learn to make a handy cup using only a sheet of paper!
Begin with a square piece of paper and follow the instructions below.

Step 1:

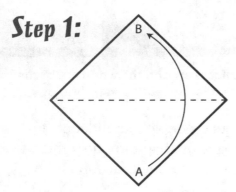

Fold your square on the diagonal,
matching up corners **A** and **B**.

Step 2:

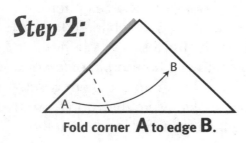

Fold corner **A** to edge **B**.

Step 3:

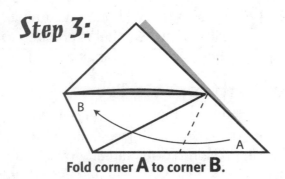

Fold corner **A** to corner **B**.

Step 4:

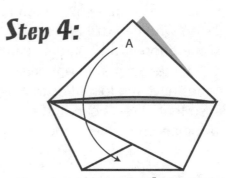

Take the top flap (flap **A**) and fold down
toward you. Turn the cup over and repeat
the step with the other remaining flap.

Step 5:

Gently push the sides in to form your cup.
If you followed the instructions above, your cup
should look like this and be able to hold water.
Enjoy!

54

Ashton Hammerheads Schedule
for September 2015

Sunday	Monday	Tuesday	Wednesday	Thursday	Friday	Saturday
		1 vs. E.C. Thunder	**2** vs. E.C. Thunder 12:30 P.M.	**3**	**4** vs. Plymouth Bobcats	**5** vs. Plymouth Bobcats 12:15 P.M.
6 vs. Plymouth Bobcats	**7** vs. Tulsa Knights	**8** vs. Tulsa Knights	**9** vs. Tulsa Knights 12:30 P.M.	**10**	**11** vs. Winston Bears 3:00 P.M.	**12** vs. Winston Bears
13 vs. Winston Bears 12:00 P.M.	**14** vs. Lake City Buffaloes 7:00 P.M.	**15** vs. Lake City Buffaloes 7:00 P.M.	**16** vs. Lake City Buffaloes 1:30 P.M.	**17**	**18** vs. Bridgeport Pirates	**19** vs. Bridgeport Pirates 1:00 P.M.
20 vs. Bridgeport Pirates 1:00 P.M.	**21**	**22** vs. Tri-City Cyclones	**23** vs. Tri-City Cyclones	**24** vs. Tri-City Cyclones 12:15 P.M.	**25** vs. Hudson Hackers 1:00 P.M.	**26** vs. Hudson Hackers
27 vs. Hudson Hackers 1:15 P.M.	**28**	**29** vs. Tulsa Knights 2:00 P.M.	**30** vs. Tulsa Knights			

Hammerheads T-shirt day
(free T-shirt for first 1,500 fans)

Hammerheads cap day
(free baseball cap for all fans under age 15)

League Championship ticket raffle
(all fans entered into a drawing for four free tickets to the League Championship game)

▢ = **Hammerheads home game** ▢ = **Hammerheads away game**

All games begin at 6:00 P.M. unless otherwise indicated.
All home games are played at Hammerhead Stadium, Rockville Center.

Tickets $25

Blue Line Train Schedule

Jackson St. to Rockville Center

Station Name	TRAIN 1 Arrive / Depart	TRAIN 2 Arrive / Depart	Station Notes
Jackson St.	11:15 / 11:20	1:25 / 1:30	Jackson St. Apartments
23rd St.	11:40 / 11:45	1:50 / 1:55	
Broadway/34th St.	12:00 / 12:05	2:10 / 2:15	Fruitvale Mall
Oakland Ave.	12:15 / 12:20	2:25 / 2:30	
Rockville Center	12:30	2:40	Hammerhead Stadium

A.M. Trains

P.M. Trains

Rockville Center to Jackson St.

Station Name	TRAIN 1 Arrive / Depart	TRAIN 2 Arrive / Depart	Station Notes
Rockville Center	2:30 / 2:35	3:20 / 3:25	Hammerhead Stadium
Oakland Ave.	2:45 / 2:50	3:35 / 3:40	
Broadway/34th St.	3:00 / 3:05	3:50 / 3:55	Fruitvale Mall
23rd St.	3:20 / 3:25	4:10 / 4:15	
Jackson St.	3:45	4:35	Jackson St. Apartments

A.M. Trains

P.M. Trains

TICKET PRICES:

- One-way ticket: $1.00 plus $0.50 per station stop. (Example: Oakland Ave. to 23rd St. is two station stops.)
- Round-trip ticket: $2.00 plus $0.25 per station stop. (Please keep your round-trip ticket for your return trip.)

FRONTIER FUN PARK

Home of the Legendary **PINE MOUNTAIN**

At 460 feet, Pine Mountain is the nation's highest roller coaster!
We think it's the world's greatest, most thrilling roller coaster ever!
You must be more than 4 feet tall to ride Pine Mountain.

SINGLE-DAY PASSES

	Adult (age 10+)	Child (age 3–9)
1-DAY BASIC PASS	**$40.00**	**$30.00**

Includes entry to all main attractions except for Pine Mountain roller coaster

	Adult (age 10+)	Child (age 3–9)
1-DAY PINE MOUNTAIN PASS	**$50.00**	**$40.00**

Includes entry to all main attractions, including Pine Mountain roller coaster

1-DAY PINE MOUNTAIN FAMILY PASS   **$140.00**

(Up to 2 adults and 2 children ages 3–9)
Includes entry to all main attractions, including Pine Mountain roller coaster

1-DAY PINE MOUNTAIN PLUS FAMILY PASS   **$160.00**

(Up to 2 adults and 2 children ages 3–9)
Includes entry to all main attractions, including Pine Mountain roller coaster,
plus a 20% discount on all purchases from the Frontier Cabin Outdoor Superstore

ONE-WEEK PASS

1-WEEK PINE MOUNTAIN FAMILY PASS   **$320.00**

(Up to 2 adults and 2 children ages 3–9)
Includes entry to all main attractions, including Pine Mountain roller coaster,
for 7 consecutive days

Disclaimer:
The safety of our guests is Frontier Fun Park's highest priority. However, Frontier Fun Park will not be liable for any injuries, damages, or losses that occur in connection with the Fun Park's activities.

Contents from *Survival and Loss*

— CONTENTS —

INTRODUCTION 2

CHAPTER 1. BROKEN PROMISES 3
   The Trail of Tears 3
   The Reservations 4

CHAPTER 2. LOST LAND, LOST INDEPENDENCE 6
   Coast to Coast 6
   Chief Red Cloud and the Treaty of Fort Laramie 6
   Wards of the State 8

CHAPTER 3. LIFE ON THE RESERVATIONS 10
   Lost Traditions 10
   Pushed Toward the Classroom 11
   The Boarding School Solution 12

CHAPTER 4. BOARDING SCHOOL LIFE 14
   The Journey 14
   "Before" and "After" 14
   New Names 14
   Unfamiliar Routines 16
   Runaways 17
   Keeping Culture Alive 17

CHAPTER 5. LESSONS AND LEARNING 18
   Entering a Strange World 18
   New Skills 20

CHAPTER 6. BOARDING SCHOOLS IN QUESTION 22
   A Good Investment? 22
   The Meriam Report 22
   Closed for Good 22

CHAPTER 7. LONG-TERM EFFECTS 24
   Effects on the Students 24
   Effects on Native American Culture as a Whole 25
   Hope for the Future 26

APPENDIX A. THE WORD "NO" 27

APPENDIX B. MAJOR EVENTS IN NATIVE AMERICAN HISTORY 28

GLOSSARY 29

INDEX 30

1. Broken Promises

THE TRAIL OF TEARS

In the 1800s, European settlers flooded into the United States. As they began building new lives for themselves—mining for gold and building towns, farms, canals, and railroads—they took over more and more land.

In 1836, the U.S. government tried to resolve its "Indian problem" by giving the eastern Native American tribes two years to move westward from their homelands. If these tribes didn't move within the two-year period, they would be forced to leave. While many tribes had little choice but to go, some tribes fought against removal.

For example, only 2,000 of the 18,000 Native Americans in the area known today as Georgia had moved by the end of the two years. In 1838, government soldiers force-marched the Cherokee and other tribes from Georgia all the

Painting by Robert Lindneux, Woolaroc Museum, Bartlesville, Oklahoma

"It is with sorrow we are forced by the white man to quit the scenes of our childhood. We bid farewell to it and all we hold dear."

—Charles Hicks, Cherokee chief

(continues)

1. Broken Promises

way to present-day Oklahoma. During the long, difficult journey of more than 1,000 miles, about 4,000 people became ill and died. This journey became known as the Trail of Tears.

Present-day Oklahoma was set aside as Native American territory. However, this land was different from the land the eastern tribes were used to. The crops they had grown in the East didn't grow on the new land, there were few wild animals to hunt, and the plants and geography were unfamiliar. The Native Americans had no way to rebuild the life they had built for themselves in the East. Even as the tribes struggled to survive in Oklahoma, much of the land they had been given was taken back by the U.S. government as the population of white settlers grew.

THE RESERVATIONS

The plains (or western) tribes were also struggling to survive. When gold was discovered in California in 1849, a flood of white settlers began traveling west hoping to make their fortunes, passing through Native American hunting grounds on the way. Tensions began to build as the two peoples crossed paths.

Unlike Native Americans, the settlers were not respectful of the land. They cut down many trees and hunted too many animals. There were so many violent **confrontations** between Native Americans and settlers that the U.S. government became worried that there might be a full-scale war.

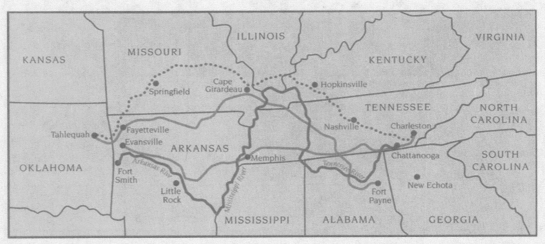

Cherokee Removal Routes This map shows four different Cherokee removal routes. Most of the tribes walked these routes. Some traveled by a combination of wagon, boat, and horse.

2. Lost Land, Lost Independence

WARDS OF THE STATE

In 1871, all Native American tribes lost their right to sign treaties when the U.S. government declared that it no longer recognized the tribes as nations, but instead thought of Native Americans as "wards of the state." A ward of the state is a person who cannot take responsibility for himself or herself, such as a young child.

U.S. troops and government agents took control of the reservations. The agents distributed rations of food and secondhand clothes. The Native Americans were treated as if they could not care for themselves, and on the reservations, this became true. The Native Americans were forced to depend on the government because they no longer had the resources they needed to make a living. They were a long way from the land they knew.

(continues)

The reservations were on land that none of the settlers wanted. Many of the tribes had never learned to farm in the European American way, and the poor-quality soil on the reservations made it impossible to learn. So many bison had been killed to make way for the building of the railroad that there were not enough bison to hunt. The tribes could not feed themselves or their families.

Now the United States had a different kind of "Indian problem." Native Americans were no longer **self-sufficient**. If they were not able to provide for themselves on the reservations, their children would not learn how to provide for themselves, either.

Marjorie C. Leggitt

Excerpt from *Survival and Loss* (3)

1. Broken Promises

way to present-day Oklahoma. During the long, difficult journey of more than 1,000 miles, about 4,000 people became ill and died. This journey became known as the Trail of Tears.

Present-day Oklahoma was set aside as Native American territory. However, this land was different from the land the eastern tribes were used to. The crops they had grown in the East didn't grow on the new land, there were few wild animals to hunt, and the plants and geography were unfamiliar. The Native Americans had no way to rebuild the life they had built for themselves in the East. Even as the tribes struggled to survive in Oklahoma, much of the land they had been given was taken back by the U.S. government as the population of white settlers grew.

THE RESERVATIONS

The plains (or western) tribes were also struggling to survive. When gold was discovered in California in 1849, a flood of white settlers began traveling west hoping to make their fortunes, passing through Native American hunting grounds on the way. Tensions began to build as the two peoples crossed paths.

Unlike Native Americans, the settlers were not respectful of the land. They cut down many trees and hunted too many animals. There were so many violent **confrontations** between Native Americans and settlers that the U.S. government became worried that there might be a full-scale war.

Cherokee Removal Routes   This map shows four different Cherokee removal routes. Most of the tribes walked these routes. Some traveled by a combination of wagon, boat, and horse.

(continues)

Native Americans fought hard to combat the sudden flood of settlers into their homelands.

In 1851, in an attempt to keep the Native Americans out of the settlers' way, the U.S. Congress introduced the Indian **Appropriation** Act. The act said the Lakota, Cheyenne, Arapaho, Crow, and other western tribes would live on areas of land known as reservations until they stopped attacking the settlers. Each tribe was given a specific piece of land. The U.S. government agreed that the tribes would receive a yearly payment for as long as they lived on the reservations, but soon the U.S. government reduced the number of years for payment. In some cases, the U.S. government had promised the same land to more than one tribe, and fights broke out between the tribes as they competed for water, game, and land. As more and more settlers moved westward in search of gold and land, the government also made the reservations smaller.

4. Boarding School Life

THE JOURNEY

In October 1879, 82 boys and girls began their journey from South Dakota to Carlisle Indian Industrial School. When they boarded the train, they were told that they were "going to school." They didn't know why they were taken from their homes, how far they would travel, or whether they would see their families again. One boy, named Ota Kte, thought that they were going to be killed. However, believing that he was doing something brave for his tribe, Ota Kte boarded the train with the others.

The long, noisy train ride was the first of many strange experiences for the children. Whenever the train stopped in a city, crowds of people stared at them, curious to see the "wild" children. The children huddled inside, frightened and confused.

"BEFORE" AND "AFTER"

When the hungry, exhausted children arrived at Carlisle, Captain Pratt's program began immediately. First, the children were photographed. Next, they were stripped of their traditional clothing, including the special beaded necklaces their parents had given them to mark an important journey or change in their lives. Everything was placed in a pile and burned. The children were then scrubbed in hot baths and given uniforms to wear. The children were used to wearing loose clothing and soft moccasins on their feet, so the stiff collars, belts, and boots made them feel trapped and **anxious**. They felt as if they were locked in cages.

Captain Pratt also thought that the boys' long hair made them look like savages and had it cut short. Traditionally, the only time Native Americans cut their hair was during times of **mourning**. The children wailed as it was cut.

Finally, with their new clothes and short hair, the children were photographed again.

NEW NAMES

At the school, the children were **immersed** in English. Immersion is a way of teaching foreign languages in which teachers and students use only the foreign language. The children were forbidden to speak their native languages at any time. They had no way to express their feelings of homesickness and confusion because they didn't know the English words for their thoughts and feelings. If Native American

Marjorie C. Leggitt

(continues)

Pratt wanted to show "before" and "after" photographs to people so that he could prove that he had "civilized" the children.

(continues)

4. Boarding School Life

What's in a Name?

Native American names are given to honor what a person has done or what qualities he or she has. For example, the Cherokee name *Ayita* means "first to dance" and the Sioux name *Hantaywee* means "faithful." *Ota Kte*, meaning "plenty kill," had been given his name to honor his father's skills as a warrior.

children spoke their native languages at school, they were made to wash their own mouths with soap.

As part of their English language immersion, the children chose English names for themselves from a list on a chalkboard. The names belonged to U.S. presidents and other important people, but the scribbles on the chalkboard meant nothing to the children. With new names and appearances, the children no longer felt like themselves.

UNFAMILIAR ROUTINES

At mealtimes, the children had to march like soldiers to long dining tables. They waited for a bell to ring before sitting down to eat. The children had never sat at tables or used knives, forks, and napkins before. Most had never eaten such foods as flour or sugar.

The children became sick because of their new diet and because they were living in such close quarters. Diseases then spread quickly in the crowded, drafty **dormitories**. The children had no **immunity** against illnesses such as measles, mumps, and influenza. In the first year, 6 boys died and 15 children were sent home ill.

As bad as the days were, the nights were worse. As one Sioux woman, Zitkala-Sa, later wrote, "Not a soul came to comfort me. I was only one of many little animals driven by a herder." The dormitories were very strange to the children. At home, there was no furniture, and families slept together in round **tepees** and lodges, but at Carlisle, beds were arranged in long rows, and the children were forbidden to speak to one another.

Marjorie C. Leggitt

6. Boarding Schools in Question

A GOOD INVESTMENT?

The Carlisle school opened in 1879. Initially, the U.S. government saw Carlisle as a great success. Other boarding schools for Native American children began to open. By 1902, there were 25 boarding schools in 15 states, and very few Native American students were left attending day schools on the reservations. Almost 10,000 children were enrolled in boarding schools.

However, despite the $45 million spent between 1880 and 1900 to "educate" about 20,000 Native American children in the ways of European American society, very few students actually graduated from the schools. For example, only 8 percent of the students who attended Carlisle ever graduated. Many students ran away, and many of those who remained were not educated—or Americanized—in the way supporters of the schools had hoped. Some people in the U.S. government began to question how well the schools really worked.

THE MERIAM REPORT

In 1928, the U.S. government could see that many of its Native American policies had failed. A researcher named Lewis Meriam was sent to prepare a report about the conditions on Native American reservations and in boarding schools. Meriam led a team of experts, including scientists, historians, teachers, and lawyers. They found that in all areas of life, Native Americans were suffering—especially children in boarding schools. Just a few of the findings in Meriam's report, called "The Problem of Indian Administration," were:

- Health conditions in boarding schools were terrible.

- A diet lacking in nutrients was causing children to become ill.

- Schools considered work such as farming and cleaning to be more important than classroom education.

- Schools followed **rigid** routines that stopped children from being creative.

- Lessons should include Native American subjects to help students feel more comfortable in unfamiliar classrooms.

CLOSED FOR GOOD

At the time of the Meriam Report, almost 80 percent of Native American school-aged children were in boarding schools. The report was embarrassing for the U.S. government because it showed that children should not be taken away from their homes to be educated.

(continues)

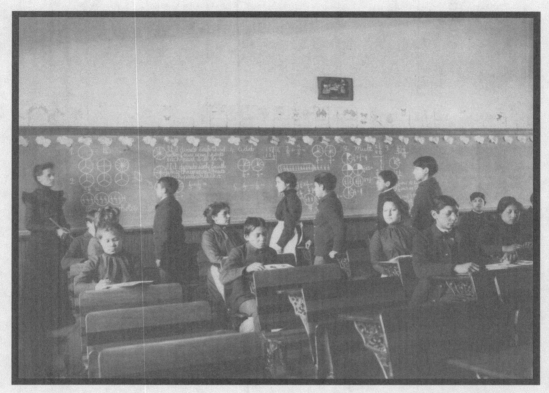

The strict routines and teaching style of boarding schools had done little to help Native American students learn. This photograph shows students during a mathematics class at Carlisle.

Meriam and his team concluded that Native American children should instead attend day schools or public schools that would keep them connected to their families and communities. By the 1930s, most of the boarding schools, including Carlisle, had been closed for good.

Double-entry Journal

About *Survival and Loss*

Text Structure	Examples from the Text
sequence	
cause/effect	
compare/contrast	

Think, Pair, Write

About *A River Ran Wild*

Name:

> What is important to know or remember from the story? Share your thinking with your partner. Then write your ideas below.

_____

_____

_____

_____

_____

_____

_____

_____

_____

_____

_____

_____

_____

_____

_____

_____

from *A River Ran Wild* (1)
by Lynne Cherry

At the start of the new century, an industrial revolution came to the Nashua's banks and waters. Many new machines were invented. Some spun thread from wool and cotton. Others wove the thread into cloth. Some machines turned wood to pulp, and others made the pulp into paper. Leftover pulp and dye and fiber was dumped into the Nashua River, whose swiftly flowing current washed away the waste.

from *A River Ran Wild* (2)
by Lynne Cherry

These were times of much excitement, times of "progress" and "invention." Factories along the Nashua River made new things of new materials. Telephones and radios and other things were made of plastics. Chemicals and plastic waste were also dumped into the river. Soon the Nashua's fish and wildlife grew sick from this pollution.

The paper mills continued to pollute the Nashua's waters. Every day for many decades pulp was dumped into the Nashua, and as the pulp clogged up the river, it began to run more slowly.

As the pulp decomposed, bad smells welled up from the river. People who lived near the river smelled its stench and stayed far from it. Each day as the mills dyed paper red, green, blue, and yellow, the Nashua ran whatever color the paper was dyed.

Soon no fish lived in the river. No birds stopped on their migration. No one could see pebbles shining up through murky water. The Nashua was dark and dirty. The Nashua was slowly dying.

A River Ran Wild by Lynne Cherry tells the story of the Nashua River, a river that ran wild through forests filled with animals. A group of native people settled near the river and named it Nash-a-way, which means River with the Pebbled Bottom. These people lived in peace until white settlers arrived and began taking more of the land for themselves. The two groups fought and the native people were driven from the land.

Over the years, factories were built that polluted the river, killing the animals and turning the water murky and smelly. After years of neglect, two people decided to do something to save the Nashua River. Their efforts led to the passing of new laws that stopped factories from polluting the river. Slowly the Nashua's current cleaned the river, and once again, a river runs wild.

Summary of *Richard Wright and the Library Card*

The book *Richard Wright and the Library Card* by William Miller tells about an important time in the life of Richard Wright, an African American author. Richard Wright grew up in the American South during segregation. As a child, he loved stories. But his family was poor and did not have much money for books. Because of segregation, Richard could not check books out of the library, either.

When Richard was 17, he left home and got a job in Memphis. His plan was to earn enough money to move north and start a new life. At his new job, Richard became friendly with a white man named Jim Falk. One day Richard asked Jim if he could use his library card to check out books for himself, and Jim agreed. Richard had to pretend the books were for Jim, but he managed to check them out.

Reading the library books changed Richard Wright's life. They opened new worlds of ideas and emotions. Richard knew he would never be the same. For the first time, he truly felt free.

Mrs. Buell

by Jean Little

Section 1

For years and years, for what seems like forever, I've gone to BUELLS when I had a dime to spare. It's a run-down, not very clean corner store. Kids go there mostly, for licorice and bubble gum and jawbreakers and Popsicles and comic books and cones. She only has three flavors and the cones taste stale. Still, she'll sell you one scoop for fifteen cents. It's not a full scoop but it's cheaper than anywhere else. It's the only place I know where a kid can spend one penny.

Mrs. Buell is run-down too, and a grouch. She never smiles or asks you how you are. Little kids are scared to go in there alone. We laugh at them but really, we understand. We felt it too, when we were smaller and had to face her towering behind the counter.

Section 2

She was always the same except that once. I tripped going in, and fell and scraped my knee. It hurt so much that I couldn't move for a second. I was winded too, and I

(continues)

had to gasp for breath. I managed not to cry out but I couldn't keep back the tears.

Mrs. Buell is big but she moved like lightning. She hauled a battered wooden chair out from behind the curtain that hung across the back. Then, without a word, she picked me up and sat me down on it. We were alone in the store but I wasn't afraid. Her hands, scooping me up, had been work-roughened; hard but kind.

She still didn't speak. Instead, she took a bit of rag out of her sweater pocket, bent down and wiped the smear of blood off my knee. The rag looked grayish but her hands were gentle. I think she liked doing it. Then she fetched a Band-Aid and stuck it on.

"Does it still sting?" she asked, speaking at last, in a voice I'd never heard her use before.

Section 3

I shook my head. And she smiled. At least I think she did. It only lasted a fraction of a second. And I wasn't looking straight at her.

(continues)

Mrs. Buell *(continued)*

At that moment Johnny Tresano came in with one nickel clutched in his fist. He was so intent on the candies he hardly noticed me. He stood and stood, trying to decide.

"Make up your mind or take yourself off," she growled.

She had gone back behind the counter. I waited for her to look at me again so that I could thank her. But when he left she turned her back and began moving things around on the shelves. I had meant to buy some jujubes but I lost my nerve. After all, everybody knew she hated kids. She was probably sorry now that she'd fixed my knee. I slunk out without once opening my mouth.

Yet, whenever I looked down and saw the Band-Aid, I felt guilty. As soon as one corner came loose, I pulled it off and threw it away. I didn't go near the store for weeks.

Section 4

She was terribly fat. She got so hot in summer that her hair hung down in wet strings and her clothes looked limp. In winter she wore the same sweater every day, a man's gray one, too big, with the

(continues)

sleeves pushed up. They kept slipping down and she'd shove them back a million times a day. Yet she never rolled up the cuffs to make them shorter.

She never took days off. She was always there. We didn't like her or hate her. We sort of knew that selling stuff to kids for a trickle of small change wasn't a job anybody would choose—especially in that poky little place with flies in summer and the door being opened all winter, letting in blasts of cold air. Even after that day when she fixed my knee, I didn't once wonder about her life.

Then I stopped at BUELLS one afternoon and she wasn't there. Instead, a man and woman I'd never laid eyes on were behind the counter sorting through stacks of stuff. They were getting some boxes down off a high shelf right then so they didn't hear me come in. I was so amazed I just stood there gawking.

Section 5

"How Ma stood this cruddy hole I'll never know!" the woman said, backing away from a cloud of dust. "Didn't she ever clean?"

(continues)

Mrs. Buell *(continued)*

"Give the subject a rest, Glo," he answered. "She's dead. She won't bother you any longer."

"I tried, Harry. You know I tried. Over and over, I told her she could move in with us. God knows I could have used a bit of cash and her help looking after those kids."

I think I must have made a sound then. Anyway, she whirled around and saw me.

"This place is closed," she snapped. "Harry, I thought I told you to lock the door. What did you want?"

I didn't want anything from her. But I still could not believe Mrs. Buell wasn't there. I stared around.

"I said we're shut. If you don't want anything, beat it," she told me.

Section 6

The minute I got home I phoned Emily. She said her mother had just read it in the paper.

"She had a daughter!" Emily said, her voice echoing my own sense of shock. "She died of a heart attack. Kate, her whole name was Katharine Ann Buell."

(continues)

Mrs. Buell *(continued)*

"Katharine," I said slowly. My name is really Katharine although only Dad calls me by it. "I can't believe it somehow."

"No," Emily said. "She was always just Mrs. Buell."

I told her about Glo and Harry. After we hung up though, I tried to imagine Mrs. Buell as a child. Instead, I saw her bending down putting that Band-Aid on my knee. Her hair had been thin on top, I remembered, and she'd had dandruff. She had tried not to hurt me. Glo's voice, talking about her, had been so cold. Had she had anyone who loved her? It seemed unlikely. Why hadn't I smiled back?

But, to be honest, something else bothered me even more. Her going had left a hole in my life. Because of it I knew, for the first time, that nothing was safe—not even the everyday, taken-for-granted background of my being. Like Mrs. Buell, pushing up her sweater sleeves and giving me my change.

Summary of

_____

_____

_____

_____

_____

_____

_____

_____

_____

_____

_____

_____

_____

_____

_____

_____

(continues)

Summary of

_____

Name:

_____

_____

_____

_____

_____

_____

_____

_____

_____

_____

_____

_____

_____

_____

_____

 of "Mrs. Buell"

In the story "Mrs. Buell" by Jean Little, a girl named Kate tells about Mrs. Buell, a grouchy woman who owns a store in Kate's neighborhood. One day Kate trips and falls in the store, and Mrs. Buell picks her up and puts a Band-Aid on her knee. Kate is surprised to find out that Mrs. Buell has a nice side. She doesn't think about Mrs. Buell much after that until she goes into the store one day and discovers that Mrs. Buell has died. Kate learns that the old woman had a daughter and a whole other life that Kate knew nothing about. Kate realizes that she never tried to get to know Mrs. Buell. She also realizes that "nothing was safe" in her life. Even the everyday things that she takes for granted can suddenly disappear.

I would recommend this story because it made me think about my own life and how I sometimes overlook people. In the story, Kate doesn't pay much attention to Mrs. Buell, and she is sorry about that when Mrs. Buell dies. That made me think about how I need to pay more attention to people in my life and show them that I care about them.

Review of *A Picture Book of Jesse Owens*

A Picture Book of Jesse Owens by David A. Adler tells the life story of one of the greatest track-and-field stars who ever lived. Jesse Owens grew up in a poor family and was often sick when he was a boy. By junior high school, though, he had developed into a strong athlete. In high school and college, he set records in many track events, including the 220-yard dash and the high jump. In 1936, Jesse became a hero around the world when he won four gold medals at the Olympics in Berlin, Germany. After the Olympics, he made speeches and wrote books about his life and issues facing the black community. He died in 1980.

I would recommend this book. It shows how Jesse Owens overcame poverty and prejudice to become a hero. I especially liked the part where he proved to Hitler at the Olympics that African Americans, Jews, and other minorities are not inferior.

Zoo

by Edward D. Hoch

The children were always good during the month of August, especially when it began to get near the twenty-third. It was on this day that Professor Hugo's Interplanetary Zoo settled down for its annual six-hour visit to the Chicago area.

Before daybreak the crowds would form, long lines of children and adults both, each one clutching his or her dollar, and waiting with wonderment to see what race of strange creatures the Professor had brought this year.

In the past they had sometimes been treated to three-legged creatures from Venus, or tall, thin men from Mars, or even snakelike horrors from somewhere more distant. This year, as the great round ship settled slowly to earth in the huge tri-city parking area just outside of Chicago, they watched with awe as the sides slowly slid up to reveal the familiar barred cages. In them were some wild breed of nightmare—small, horselike animals that moved with quick, jerking motions and constantly chattered in a high-pitched tongue. The citizens of Earth clustered around as Professor Hugo's crew quickly collected the waiting dollars, and soon the good Professor himself made an appearance, wearing his many-colored rainbow cape and top hat. "Peoples of Earth," he called into his microphone.

The crowd's noise died down as he continued. "Peoples of Earth, this year you see a real treat for your single dollar—the little-known horse-spider people of Kaan—brought to you across a million miles of space at great expense. Gather around, study them, listen to them, tell your friends about them. But hurry! My ship can remain here only six hours!"

(continues)

Zoo *(continued)*

And the crowds slowly filed by, at once horrified and fascinated by these strange creatures that looked like horses but ran up the walls of their cages like spiders. "This is certainly worth a dollar," one man remarked, hurrying away. "I'm going home to get the wife."

All day long it went like that, until ten thousand people had filed by the barred cages set into the side of the spaceship. Then, as the six-hour limit ran out, Professor Hugo once more took microphone in hand. "We must go now, but we will return next year on this date. And if you enjoyed our zoo this year, phone your friends in other cities about it. We will land in New York tomorrow, and next week on to London, Paris, Rome, Hong Kong, and Tokyo. Then on to other worlds!"

He waved farewell to them, and as the ship rose from the ground the Earth peoples agreed that this had been the very best Zoo yet. . . .

Some two months and three planets later, the silver ship of Professor Hugo settled at last onto the familiar jagged rocks of Kaan, and the queer horse-spider creatures filed quickly out of their cages. Professor Hugo was there to say a few parting words, and then they scurried away in a hundred different directions, seeking their homes among the rocks.

In one, the she-creature was happy to see the return of her mate and offspring. She babbled a greeting in the strange tongue and hurried to embrace them. "It was a long time you were gone! Was it good?"

And the he-creature nodded. "The little one enjoyed it especially. We visited eight worlds and saw many things."

(continues)

Zoo (continued)

The little one ran up the wall of the cave. "On the place called Earth it was the best. The creatures there wear garments over their skins, and they walk on two legs."

"But isn't it dangerous?" asked the she-creature.

"No," her mate answered. "There are bars to protect us from them. We remain right in the ship. Next time you must come with us. It is well worth the nineteen commocs it costs."

And the little one nodded. "It was the very best Zoo ever. . . ."

"Zoo" by Edward D. Hoch, originally published in *Fantastic Universe*. Copyright © 1958 by Edward D. Hoch. Reprinted by permission of the Sternig & Byrne Literary Agency.

My Opinions

About "12 seconds from death"

© Center for the Collaborative Classroom

12 seconds from death

by Paul Dowswell

An icy blast roared through the Skyvan transport plane as the rear door opened to the bright blue sky. On an April morning in 1991, above the flat fields of Cambridgeshire, England, three skydivers were about to make a parachute jump they would never forget.

Richard Maynard was making his first jump. He had paid a substantial fee to plummet from 3,600m (12,000ft), strapped to Mike Smith, a skilled parachute instructor. Expecting this experience (known as a "tandem jump") to be the thrill of a lifetime, Maynard had also commissioned instructor Ronnie O'Brien to videotape him.

O'Brien leaped backwards from the plane to film Maynard and Smith's exit. The pair plunged down after him, speeding up to 290kmph (180mph) in the first 15 seconds. They soon overtook O'Brien, and Smith released a small drogue parachute to slow them down to a speed where it would be safe to open his main parachute, without it giving them a back-breaking jolt. But here disaster struck. As the chute flew from its container, the cord holding it became entangled around Smith's neck. It pulled tight, strangling him, and he quickly lost consciousness.

Watching from 90m (300ft) above, O'Brien saw the two men spinning out of control, and when the drogue parachute failed to open he knew something had gone terribly wrong. Both men were just 45 seconds from the ground. If O'Brien could not help them, they both faced certain death.

O'Brien changed from the usual spread-eagled posture of a skydiver, and swooped down through the air toward the plummeting pair, with his legs pressed tightly together and arms by his side. He

(continues)

12 seconds from death *(continued)*

How it all happened

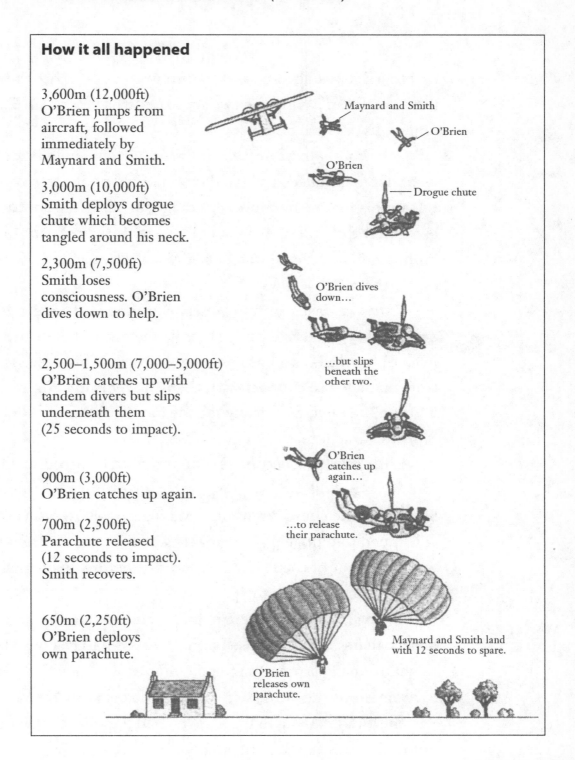

3,600m (12,000ft) O'Brien jumps from aircraft, followed immediately by Maynard and Smith.

Maynard and Smith

O'Brien

O'Brien

Drogue chute

3,000m (10,000ft) Smith deploys drogue chute which becomes tangled around his neck.

2,300m (7,500ft) Smith loses consciousness. O'Brien dives down to help.

O'Brien dives down…

…but slips beneath the other two.

2,500–1,500m (7,000–5,000ft) O'Brien catches up with tandem divers but slips underneath them (25 seconds to impact).

O'Brien catches up again…

900m (3,000ft) O'Brien catches up again.

…to release their parachute.

700m (2,500ft) Parachute released (12 seconds to impact). Smith recovers.

650m (2,250ft) O'Brien deploys own parachute.

O'Brien releases own parachute.

Maynard and Smith land with 12 seconds to spare.

(continues)

"12 seconds from death" by Paul Dowswell reproduced from *True Stories of Heroes* by permission of Usborne Publishing, 83–85 Saffron Hill, London EC1N 8RT, UK. Copyright © 2006 Usborne Publishing Ltd.

12 seconds from death (continued)

had to judge his descent very carefully. If he overshot, he would have little chance of saving the two men, but this veteran of 2,000 jumps knew what he was doing.

Positioning himself right in front of them, he quickly realized what had happened, and tried to grab hold of Smith so he could release his main parachute. But diving at the same speed was extremely difficult. O'Brien would be within arm's length of the falling men and then lurch out of reach. Then suddenly, he fell way below them.

Time was fast running out. The ground was a mere 20 seconds away and O'Brien knew he had only one more chance to save their lives. He spread his arms and legs out to slow his descent, and this time managed to connect with the pair. Whirling around and around, O'Brien searched frantically for the handle that would release Smith's parachute.

With barely 12 seconds before they hit the ground, O'Brien found the handle, and the large main chute billowed out above them. Slowed by the chute, Smith and Maynard shot away as O'Brien continued to plunge down. He released his own parachute when he was safely out of the way, a few seconds before he himself would have hit the ground.

By the time the tandem pair had landed, Smith had recovered consciousness, but collapsed almost immediately. Only then did Maynard realize something had gone wrong. Caught up in the excitement of the jump, with adrenaline coursing through his body and the wind roaring in his ears, he had had no idea that anything out of the ordinary had happened.

"12 seconds from death" by Paul Dowswell reproduced from *True Stories of Heroes* by permission of Usborne Publishing, 83–85 Saffron Hill, London EC1N 8RT, UK. Copyright © 2006 Usborne Publishing Ltd.

Double-entry Journal

My Opinions About

_____ (1)

Evidence

Opinions

The Pros and Cons of Year-round Schools

While most schools follow a traditional school calendar with a two- to three-month summer break, some schools—year-round schools—follow a different calendar and don't have a traditional summer break. In the 2006–2007 school year, there were about three thousand year-round schools in the United States educating nearly two million students. Are year-round schools better for kids? Before we examine the pros and cons of the matter, let's answer another question: What is a year-round school?

What Is a Year-round School?

Like a traditional school calendar, a year-round school calendar has about 180 days of school in a year. The difference is that year-round schools stretch out those 180 days over all twelve months of the year. Instead of the traditional two- to three-month summer vacation, year-round schools have several short breaks. The most common year-round schedule is the 45–15 plan, in which students go to school for 45 days and then get a 15-day break. They follow this pattern throughout the year.

Students who go to a year-round school avoid summer "brain drain."

Pros Let's look at some of the arguments in favor of year-round schools.

Less Summer "Brain Drain" and More Time to Learn

Research shows that over the summer students forget some of what they learned during the school year. In one study, researchers at the University of Missouri and Tennessee State University found that test scores were, on average, at least one month lower when students returned to school in the fall than when they left in the spring. Students who go to a year-round school avoid this summer "brain drain."

Do students learn more by going to school year-round? Researchers disagree on the answer to this question. Because year-round schools keep the learning process going throughout the year, some people argue that students will learn more in a year-round school. In a 2009 report on year-round school calendars and traditional school calendars, researcher Jennifer Rule wrote, "In summary, it is reasonable to conclude that students attending year-round schools were likely to perform as well if not better than their peers in traditional 9-month programs. . . ."

Schools Save Money

Year-round schooling can save money. Schools on a year-round schedule can "multitrack" students so that while some of them are in school, others are on break. This means schools can enroll up to 33 percent more students. This multitrack system reduces the need for building new schools due to overcrowding. For example, Florida's Marion County school system estimates saving more than twelve million dollars in construction costs because the district switched to multitrack year-round schooling.

More Flexibility for Families

The traditional summer break can be a burden on a family's time and finances. Most parents cannot take time off from work for two or three months to be with their kids, and child care is expensive. The shorter, more frequent breaks in year-round schools give working parents more flexibility in deciding when to take time off and how to provide child care.

 Now let's look at some of the arguments against year-round schools.

No Proven Gains in Academic Achievement

An important argument for year-round schools is that attending school year-round will likely lead to gains in academic achievement. In fact, although many studies have been done on the impact of year-round schools and traditional schools on student achievement, the results are inconclusive. Some studies show gains; others do not. For example, a study released in 2013 showed that there was little evidence of increased achievement by students in year-round schools.

No Much-needed Summer Break

The longer summer vacation of a traditional school calendar gives students lots of time to unwind, connect with friends, and be with their families. It provides older students with opportunities to find summer work and earn money for college. It gives younger children time to attend summer camps—time that students who attend year-round schools do not have. One expert, Dr. Peter Scales, says, "The biggest plus of camp is that camps help young people discover and explore their talents, interests, and values. Most schools don't satisfy all these needs. Kids who have had these kinds of [camp] experiences end up being healthier and have [fewer] problems. . . ."

"Year-round" Equals "Expensive"

Some school districts have found that switching to year-round schooling has cost them more money. Year-round schools have to provide air-conditioning and other utilities all year long, and there is more maintenance to do because buildings are being used more. In her first year as superintendent of Tempe Union High School District in Tempe, Arizona, Shirley Miles won praise for eliminating the high school's year-round calendar and its added costs.

Are year-round schools a good idea? There are strong arguments to be made on both sides of the question. What do you think?

Summer break gives kids time to reconnect with friends.

YEAR-ROUND SCHOOL
I'm for It

By Chance T., Imperial, NE

Summer is awesome, but after a couple of months, it's time for school again. You walk into class that first day back and hear, "Pop quiz! Let's see what you know." It's always difficult to start a new school year after a long summer break, but if you go to a year-round school, that first day back is a lot easier. I believe all kids should go to year-round schools.

One argument against year-round schooling is that you and your family can't take long trips over summer vacation. True, you might not get to take a three-week trip, but who does? Typically, a family vacation is a week or two. If you go to a year-round school, you can take three, or even four, short trips during the year—one during each break. You can see more places that way.

A study showed that after completing a year of year-round school, 79 percent of students were in favor of the year-round calendar.

I know the idea of going to school year-round sounds pretty awful to some of you, but kids who go to year-round schools seem to like it. Elisabeth Palmer and Amy Bemis, authors of *Year-Round Education*, have done research on year-round schools. They said, "The results indicated that after one year of experiencing a 60–15 calendar [60 days of school followed by 15 days of vacation], students felt more positively about year-round education."

Palmer and Bemis found that 53 percent of students in the study "favored year-round education during the summer before implementation, while 79 percent favored it at the end of the first year." That means that after the kids in the study tried a year-round school schedule for a year, more of them were for it!

Another argument against year-round schooling is that there are fewer days of learning because there are so many breaks. Just when you're getting excited about learning something, it's time for a break. But if you look closely, you will see that actual learning time is the same in a year-round school, and after each break, the students are refreshed and more ready to listen and learn.

Also, students in year-round schools don't have to relearn what they forgot over the summer. Donald Beggs, a former assistant professor at Southern Illinois University, and Albert Hieronymus, a former professor at the University of Iowa, researched summer learning and found that there were consistent losses in math and language skills during the traditional summer break.

I feel that year-round schooling would benefit all students. Kids would have more vacations and would learn more because they wouldn't have to relearn the information they had forgotten after long summer breaks.

Year-round schooling can provide families with more opportunities to spend time together throughout the year.

Year-round School
I'm Against It

By Anonymous, Temecula, CA

During the summer, most kids are out of school and enjoying time at home or on a family trip. But some kids go to school all summer long—and it's not because they have to go to summer school. It's because their school is on a year-round schedule. When my friends in year-round schools tell me they can't spend time with me during my summer break because they're in school, I'm sad and disappointed.

In the 2011–2012 school year, more than three thousand schools in the United States followed a year-round schedule. According to a 2010 survey conducted by Wake County Public School System in North Carolina, about 45 percent of parents said that schools should be on a year-round schedule, and about 49 percent said that they should not. Year-round schooling has its pros and cons. I'm against year-round schools for several reasons.

First, family vacations are usually planned for the summer break. Typically, this is a time to see relatives, relax, spend time as a family, and have fun. Year-round school schedules limit the time families have for summer vacations. Kids in year-round schools also don't have time to go to summer camp. At camp, kids get to be outdoors, make new friends, and learn nature facts. If schools everywhere were on a year-round schedule, summer camps might cease to exist.

Year-round schooling limits the time kids have for family summer vacations and summer camp.

The school year is filled with tests, quizzes, homework, and studying. After all that hard work, students deserve a summer break to relax and refresh. There are some who argue that kids forget things they have learned during a long summer break. I think they're wrong because kids still use their brains during the summer. A 2011 study by the RAND Corporation showed that students who went to a summer camp or participated in another type of educational summer program not only had fun but also kept information in their heads. If kids are concerned about forgetting what they've learned over the summer, they can ask their teachers for summer homework packets so they will be ready for next year.

Year-round school also makes it harder for students to get summer jobs. Students going to schools with traditional schedules can commit to two-month summer jobs and earn money for college. Students in year-round schools don't have the time to fill summer job openings.

Summer is to be enjoyed, not spent in classrooms. Should we change to a year-round school calendar that shortens summer vacation? The answer, I think, is that we should not.

There are many activities that engage kids' brains over the summer.

Double-entry Journal

My Opinions About

_____ (2)

Opinions

Evidence

Summer Reading List

Name:

List the books you would like to read this summer. For each book, write the title, the author's name, and a few words to remind you what the book is about.

Book Title	Author	Reminder

of *The Legend of Sleepy Hollow*

by Jennifer B. (age 12)

In *The Legend of Sleepy Hollow* by Washington Irving, Ichabod Crane has just arrived to Sleepy Hollow and has met a lot of people. Those people have told Ichabod the legend of Sleepy Hollow.

This legend is about a headless horseman who goes around cutting other people's heads in search of his own. This legend scared Ichabod every time it was told. Ichabod Crane had fallen in love with Katrina, a very rich girl, a couple of weeks after he arrived to Sleepy Hollow. One day Ichabod was invited to Katrina's party, and before the party was over a woman started to say the legend of Sleepy Hollow and at the end she said the only way you can escape the headless horseman is by crossing the bridge. That night Ichabod and his horse ran as fast as they could to reach their house. Finally he was up to the bridge that meant that he was near his house. Then something got in his way, it was the headless horseman. Did Ichabod ever escape?

I think that this book was very interesting because it was a legend about a headless horseman that lost his head in a war and since then has been looking for it by cutting other people's heads off. I recommend this book to people who like scary legends that took place a long time ago.

This story reminds me of "Bloody Mary" because they are both scary and they are both legends. What makes this story more scary is that it has been told for more than 100 years and it has been told by people who are already dead.

Things to Include in My Book Review

Name: _____

Book title: _____

Author: _____

_____

_____

_____

_____

_____

_____

_____

_____

_____

_____

_____

_____

_____

_____

_____

Review of

_____

(continues)

Review of

_____

Name:

Thoughts About My Reading Life

Name: _____

What are some of your favorite kinds of books now? Why?

_____

_____

_____

Where is your favorite place to read?

_____

_____

_____

What does the word *reading* mean to you?

_____

_____

_____

When you don't understand something you are reading, what do you do?

_____

_____

_____

What kinds of books did you read for the first time this year? What topics did you read about for the first time?

_____

_____

Reading Log

Reading Log

Name:

Date	Title	Author
Comment:		
Comment:		
Comment:		
Comment:		
Comment:		
Comment:		
Comment:		

Date	Title	Author
Comment:		
Comment:		
Comment:		
Comment:		
Comment:		
Comment:		
Comment:		

Reading Log

Name:

Date	Title	Author
Comment:		
Comment:		
Comment:		
Comment:		
Comment:		
Comment:		
Comment:		

Date	Title	Author
Comment:		
Comment:		
Comment:		
Comment:		
Comment:		
Comment:		
Comment:		

Reading Log

Date	Title	Author

Comment:

Comment:

Comment:

Comment:

Comment:

Comment:

Comment:

Date	Title	Author
Comment:		
Comment:		
Comment:		
Comment:		
Comment:		
Comment:		
Comment:		

Reading Log

Name:

Date	Title	Author

Comment:

Comment:

Comment:

Comment:

Comment:

Comment:

Comment:

Date	Title	Author
Comment:		
Comment:		
Comment:		
Comment:		
Comment:		
Comment:		
Comment:		

Reading Log

Name:

Date	Title	Author

Comment:

Comment:

Comment:

Comment:

Comment:

Comment:

Date	Title	Author

Comment:

Comment:

Comment:

Comment:

Comment:

Comment:

Comment:

Reading Log

Name:

Date	Title	Author

Comment:

Comment:

Comment:

Comment:

Comment:

Comment:

Comment:

Date	Title	Author

Comment:

Comment:

Comment:

Comment:

Comment:

Comment:

Comment:

Reading Log

Name:

Date	Title	Author

Comment:

Comment:

Comment:

Comment:

Comment:

Comment:

Comment:

Date	Title	Author
Comment:		
Comment:		
Comment:		
Comment:		
Comment:		
Comment:		
Comment:		

Reading Log

Name:

Date	Title	Author
Comment:		
Comment:		
Comment:		
Comment:		
Comment:		
Comment:		
Comment:		

Reading Journal

Reading Journal

Name: _____ Date: _____

_____

_____

_____

_____

_____

_____

_____

_____

_____

_____

_____

_____

_____

_____

_____

Reading Journal

Name: _____   Date: _____

_____

_____

_____

_____

_____

_____

_____

_____

_____

_____

_____

_____

_____

_____

Reading Journal

Name: _____   Date: _____

_____

_____

_____

_____

_____

_____

_____

_____

_____

_____

_____

_____

_____

_____

_____

Reading Journal

Name: _____ Date: _____

_____

_____

_____

_____

_____

_____

_____

_____

_____

_____

_____

_____

_____

_____

_____

Reading Journal

Name: _____   Date: _____

_____

_____

_____

_____

_____

_____

_____

_____

_____

_____

_____

_____

_____

_____

_____

_____

Reading Journal

Name: _____ Date: _____

_____

_____

_____

_____

_____

_____

_____

_____

_____

_____

_____

_____

_____

_____

_____

Reading Journal

Name: _____ Date: _____

_____
_____
_____
_____
_____
_____
_____
_____
_____
_____
_____
_____
_____
_____
_____
_____

Reading Journal

Name: _____ Date: _____

_____

_____

_____

_____

_____

_____

_____

_____

_____

_____

_____

_____

_____

_____

_____

Reading Journal

Name: _____ Date: _____

_____

_____

_____

_____

_____

_____

_____

_____

_____

_____

_____

_____

_____

_____

_____

_____

Reading Journal

Name: _____ Date: _____

_____

_____

_____

_____

_____

_____

_____

_____

_____

_____

_____

_____

_____

_____

_____

_____

_____

Reading Journal

Name: _____   Date: _____

_____

_____

_____

_____

_____

_____

_____

_____

_____

_____

_____

_____

_____

_____

Reading Journal

Name: _____   Date: _____

_____

_____

_____

_____

_____

_____

_____

_____

_____

_____

_____

_____

_____

_____

_____

_____

Reading Journal

Name: _____ Date: _____

_____

_____

_____

_____

_____

_____

_____

_____

_____

_____

_____

_____

_____

_____

_____

Reading Journal

Name: _____ Date: _____

_____

_____

_____

_____

_____

_____

_____

_____

_____

_____

_____

_____

_____

_____

_____

_____

_____

_____

_____

Reading Journal

Name: _____ Date: _____

_____

_____

_____

_____

_____

_____

_____

_____

_____

_____

_____

_____

_____

_____

_____

Reading Journal

Name: _____ Date: _____

_____

_____

_____

_____

_____

_____

_____

_____

_____

_____

_____

_____

_____

_____

_____

_____

_____

Reading Journal

Name: _____ Date: _____

_____

_____

_____

_____

_____

_____

_____

_____

_____

_____

_____

_____

_____

_____

_____

_____

_____

_____

Reading Journal

Name: _____   Date: _____

_____

_____

_____

_____

_____

_____

_____

_____

_____

_____

_____

_____

_____

_____

_____

_____

_____

_____

Reading Journal

Name: _____ Date: _____

_____

_____

_____

_____

_____

_____

_____

_____

_____

_____

_____

_____

_____

_____

_____

_____

_____